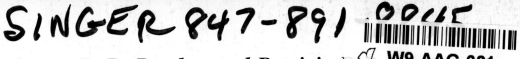

R. D. Bartlett and Patricia P. Bartlett

Frogs, Toads, and Treefrogs

Everything about Selection, Care,
Nutrition, Breeding, and Behavior

With 87 Color Photographs by R. D. Bartlett

Illustrations by Patricia P. Bartlett,
Michele Earle-Bridges, and Tom Kerr

BARRON'S

Cover Photos

Front cover: *Litoria caerulea*
Inside front cover: *Hyla versicolor*
Inside back cover: *Ceratophrys cranwelli* (albino)
Back cover: top left, *Pyxicephalus adspersus;*
    top right, *Dendrobates auratus;* bottom left,
    Dendrobates reticulatus; bottom right,
    Ceratophrys ornata

All inquiries should be addressed to:
Barron's Educational Series, Inc.
250 Wireless Boulevard
Hauppauge, NY 11788

International Standard Book No. 0-8120-9156-6

Library of Congress Catalog Card No. 95-40896

Library of Congress Cataloging-in-Publication Data
Bartlett, Richard D., 1938–
    Frogs, toads, and treefrogs : everything about selection, care, nutrition, breeding, and behavior / R. D. Bartlett and Patricia P. Bartlett; illustrations by Patricia P. Bartlett.
        p.   cm.
    Includes index.
    ISBN 0-8120-9156-6
    1. Frogs as pets. 2. Toads as pets.
    3. Hylidae. I. Bartlett, Patricia Pope, 1949–   . II. Title.
    SF459.F83B37   1996
    639.3'78—dc20   95-40896
                                          CIP

Printed in Hong Kong

6789   9955   98765

About the Authors

R. D. Bartlett was born in Springfield, Massachusetts, in 1938. His interest in natural history in general and herpetology in particular has been an abiding pursuit since his preteen years.

He has participated in field studies across North and South America.

He has authored more than 400 semitechnical and popular articles and seven books on reptiles and amphibians, and he lectures extensively.

In 1978 he founded the Reptilian Breeding and Research Institute, a private facility. Since its inception more than 150 species of reptiles and amphibians have been bred at RBRI, some for the first time in the United States under captive conditions. Successes at RBRI include both common and endangered species.

Bartlett is a member of numerous herpetological and conservation organizations.

Patricia Bartlett was born in Atlanta, Georgia, and grew up in New Mexico. She received her B.S. from Colorado State University and became the editor for an outdoors book publishing firm in St. Petersburg, Florida. She worked for the science museum in Springfield, Massachusetts, and was director of the historical museum in Ft. Myers before moving to Gainesville, Florida. She is the author of eight books on natural history and historical subjects.

Important Note

Before using any of the electrical equipment described in this book, be sure to read Avoiding Electrical Accidents on page 24.

While handling anurans you may occasionally receive bites. If your skin is broken, see your physician immediately.

Many anurans, including common toads, produce defensive toxic secretions. Always wash your hands carefully with soap and water before and after handling your specimens.

Some terrarium plants may be harmful to the skin or mucous membranes of human beings. If you notice any signs of irritation, wash the area thoroughly. See your physician if the condition persists.

Always supervise children who wish to observe your frogs, toads, and treefrogs.

Contents

Preface 5
Acknowledgments 6

Understanding Anurans 7
Call Uniqueness 7
Male Competition 8
Anuran Oddities 8
Amphibian Names 10
A (Tentative) Family Tree 11
What Is Happening to the Frogs? 11

Frog Watching and Photographing 13
HOW-TO: Photographing Frogs,
   Toads, and Treefrogs 14

Caging Techniques 16
Understanding Microenvironments 16
Indoor Caging 17
Outdoor Caging 22
Cage Furnishings 22
Terrarium Cleanliness 23
Lighting and Heating 24
HOW-TO: Watering Techniques 26

Diets 27
Insects 27
Mice 31

Health Hints and Medications 32
Proper Hygiene 32
Ailments 32

Breeding Suggestions 34
Reproductive Behavior 34
Development of the Eggs 34
The Tadpoles 34
Cycling Your Frog, Toad, or Treefrog
   for Breeding 35

**The Flat-tongued Frogs: Family
   Discoglossidae 40**
The Fire-bellied Toads 40

Aquarium Favorites: Family Pipidae 44
The Tongueless Frogs 44

Burrowers: Family Pelobatidae 50
The Spadefoots 50
The Malayan Horned Frog 51

**The Wonderful Hopping Mouths:
   Family Leptodactylidae 52**
The Horned Frogs 52
Budgett's Frog 56
The Chacoan Burrowing Frog 56
Care of Captive Ceratophrines 56

**Backyard Favorites and Exotic
   Rarities: Family Bufonidae 59**
The "Arboreal" Toads 59
The Ground-dwelling Toads 59

**Neotropical Forestland Gems:
   Family Dendrobatidae 64**
The Arrow-poison Frogs 64

**Arboreal Favorites: Family
   Hylidae 74**
Red-eyed Treefrogs 74
White's Treefrog 77
The White-lipped Treefrog 81
Other Treefrogs 82

Typical Frogs: Family Ranidae 86
The American Bullfrog 86
Pyxies 87
Other Typical Ranids 88
Madagascar's Magnificent Mantellas 90

**Tomato Frogs and Others: Family
   Microhylidae 97**
The Tomato Frogs 97
The Malayan Painted Frog 98
The Narrow-mouthed Toads and
   Sheep Frogs 98

Useful Addresses and Literature 100

Glossary 101

Index 103

Asian cascade frogs, Rana livida, *are of alert appearance. Note the toepads, which provide secure footing on mossy, river-bank boulders.*

Preface

The branch of zoology dealing with amphibians and reptiles is known as *herpetology*. That term is derived from a Greek word meaning "creeping thing." The amphibians include the salamanders, the frogs (including toads and treefrogs), and the circum-tropical, secretive, and poorly known caecilians. The reptiles include the little-known (but intensely studied) rhyncocephalians (tuataras) of New Zealand and the better-known crocodilians, lizards, snakes, turtles (including tortoises and terrapins) and the amphisbaenids, the worm lizards.

All these animals are "cold-blooded" (*poikilothermic* or *ectothermic*): they maintain their bodies at suitable temperatures through external means—usually by sunning or resting in a warmed spot. Although the amphibians are not closely related to the reptiles, both groups are frequently spoken about in the same breath.

One who studies herpetology is said to be a *herpetologist*. A *professional herpetologist*, generally formally trained, makes his or her living pursuing some aspect of the study of herpetology—i.e., zoo work, field study and interpretation, museum work, teaching, or combinations of those activities. An amateur herpetologist may or may not have formal schooling, has an avid interest in herpetology, but does not make his or her living from such interest.

Rather recently the word *herpetoculturist* has come into vogue. This term is applied to both professional and nonprofessional keepers and breeders of reptiles and amphibians.

The keeping of frogs, toads, and treefrogs in a home terrarium is a rather new aspect of the rather old hobby of herpetoculture, which is only now coming into its own. In earlier years many of these amphibians were kept merely as an offshoot of the aquarium hobby, rather than as a separate, specific interest.

Since the adults of all species lack tails, frogs, toads, and treefrogs are often referred to as tailless amphibians, or anurans. (In all of frogdom, the only species with a taillike appendage is the tailed frog, *Ascaphus truei,* which is found in two disjunct populations in the northwestern United States and immediately adjacent Canada. The "tail" is actually a protruding copulatory organ, and only the males possess it.)

Many hobbyists are introduced to the tailless amphibians through the aquarium hobby. Tropical fish stores stock at least two species of "underwater frogs," the African clawed frog, *Xenopus laevis,* and the dwarf underwater frog, *Hymenochirus curtipes.* Both are hardy community animals, at least when young. Because of its diminutive adult size, the dwarf underwater frog remains a community dweller throughout its life. In fact, in a community tank it is more likely to be the persecuted than the persecutor. That is not true of the clawed frog: What was once a compatible baby will quickly grow into a 4-inch-long (10.2 cm) eating machine dedicated to the task of ridding the aquarium of any fish that are smaller than it is. Small wonder that the (usually) unprepared aquarist often dumps this voracious, unresearched acquisition into the nearest body of water!

Today there are many species of frogs available to the interested hobbyist, and the keeping of tailless amphibians is finding more and more devotees. Many hobbyists enjoy frogs and toads because most thrive in elaborately beautiful terrariums; other enthusiasts enjoy the beasts because some frog species thrive in Spartan quarters that require little more than a few moments of care (and thought) weekly.

Frogs include such impressive species as the Australian White's treefrog; the ornate horned frog, all mouth (and more than able and willing to use it on food or finger); and the African bullfrog, big, obese, and voracious. A hobbyist may find leaf-green treefrogs with protuberant vermilion eyes, arrow-poison frogs that emulate gaudily enameled stickpins, and toads so big and warty that they appear more like a nightmare. The Surinam toad, a 6-inch-long (15.2 cm) squarish mud-colored blob with delicate-fingered forelimbs on one end and powerfully formed, immense webbed feet on the other, with tiny, lidless, stargazing eyes, has the overall appearance of having lost a battle with a steamroller.

Within these pages we will introduce to you several dozen interesting frogs, toads, and treefrogs. Some are common, some rare, some beautifully colored, others exactly the opposite; some are tree-dwellers, others burrowers, but all are currently available in America's pet trade. Together we will cover the making of a terrarium, the feeding of tailless amphibians, and the detection and treatment of diseases and disorders that might affect your "pets."

We put the word in quotation marks, for frogs, toads, and treefrogs are not pets in the strictest sense. Rather, they are interesting little animals with which you can share your home and through which you can experience a bit of the world's rapidly disappearing wilderness. We hope to arouse enough interest in these creatures to induce you to keep one or two in your home and to encourage you to see them in their natural habitats, where you can learn the whys and wherefores of their existence in the wild. We think it is essential for us to increase our knowledge about the creatures with which we share planet Earth!

Acknowledgments

Many people have helped us in many ways with this book. Bill Love and Rob MacInnes of Glades Herp Inc. and Chris McQuade of Gulf Coast Reptiles have continually gone out of their way to provide us with photographic opportunities. Peter Seigfried of Escazu, Costa Rica, found the time to get us to some of the montane streams and forest lowlands where we could observe harlequin frogs, arrow-poison frogs, and treefrogs. Ernie Wagner provided us with information regarding tomato frogs as captives and Steve Mui offered similar thoughts on White's treefrogs. Bert and Hester Langerwerf shared with us some of the details of their very successful breeding program with Chinese green gliding frogs. Ron Sayers, Dennis Cathcart, Dennie Miller, and Walt Meshaka have proved great field companions. Special acknowledgment is due our editor, Don Reis, for his suggestions, help, and encouragement. And finally, we wish to thank Fredric L. Frye, D.V.M., both for his contributions to herpetology and for his thoughtful commentary on the manuscript of this book.

Dick and Patti Bartlett

Understanding Anurans

Frogs, toads, and treefrogs are a little different from most of the other groupings of usually silent "herptiles," for the males of most frog, toad, and treefrog species have voices. Some frog-songs are as musically pleasing to the human ear as the notes of a gifted songbird, while the vocalizations of others are harsh and discordant sounds that we would prefer to avoid.

Most anurans call at night. To the tailless amphibians that produce them, the sounds are as distinctive as they are to humans, but far more important. The vocalizations not only identify species, but draw the females of the species to the breeding sites. Although it is difficult to put frog calls into words, we would like to attempt a few examples to demonstrate the diversity that exists among just a few eastern American frogs, toads, and treefrogs.

Call Uniqueness

Bullfrogs, *Rana catesbeiana*, produce a bass "jug-o-rum," usually voiced while this largest of American frogs is floating amid vegetation in deep, quiet water.

Green and bronze frogs, *Rana clamitans* ssp., sound like a loose banjo string being half-heartedly plunked several times in succession. This species may float or sit in shallow water, or sit on the shore at the edge of the water while vocalizing.

American toads, *Bufo americanus* ssp., vocalize in high-pitched, rapidly pulsed musical trills that are voiced while the males are sitting in very shallow water or on the pond's edge.

The call of the oak toad, *Bufo quercicus*, is a single, penetrating, chicklike peep voiced while the male is sitting amid emergent grasses. This, the smallest American toad, is adult at about 1 inch (25.4 mm) in length.

Gray treefrogs (two difficult-to-differentiate species) produce either a very pleasing, rather slowly pulsed musical trill (*Hyla versicolor*) or a harsher, more rapidly pulsed, less pleasing trill (*H. chrysoscelis*). Males vocalize sitting atop floating debris or clinging to emergent or pondside trees and shrubs.

The pine barrens' treefrog, *Hyla andersonii*, voices an oft-repeated, gooselike "quonk." Calling sites may be amid emergent grasses or tangles of vines and briars near pondside trees.

Thus we have a range of vocalizations that sound like plunks, trills, peeps, quonks, and "jug-o-rums." The call of each species is distinctively different from that voiced by other species in the same ecological niche. For instance, in New England while an American toad voices its melodious trill, a rather similar Fowler's toad nearby emits a harsh wail. In Florida a beautiful green treefrog voices its ringing honks while a slightly smaller squirrel treefrog churrs out a call often likened to the barks of an irate gray squirrel. In Arizona a Couch's spadefoot toad produces a plaintive groan while a slightly smaller western spadefoot sitting next to it voices a hoarse snore. All of these voices are immediately recognizable as different by both frogs and humans.

Identifying anurans by call: The ability of birders to recognize not only

Although called "green frog," many Rana clamitans melanota *are actually of the bronzy color that is usually associated with the more southerly subspecies,* R. c. clamitans.

the songs, but the incidental tweets and peeps of their avian quarry has long been acknowledged. The calls of frogs and toads are also easily learned; and since most anurans call at night, following the calls to their source will often divulge populations of tailless amphibians that would otherwise go unseen. For those who wish to identify more frog and toad calls, several records and tapes exist. The eastern species are especially well

The Pine barrens treefrog, Hyla andersonii, *is, arguably, the most beautiful treefrog of the United States. It is no longer a common species.*

covered. These recordings are often available through natural history museums or conservation organizations.

Male Competition

It is the males that arrive first at the breeding sites to seek and stake out the best locations. Once ensconced they must strive to protect their sites and attract females of their species through vocalizations. It is now known that breeding among tailless amphibians is not the random encounter once thought. Rather, a selection process that favors the largest and the loudest draws the females to the fittest males. In their quest, the female frogs, toads, and treefrogs, once thought to be complacent in the breeding process, are now known to rebuff the amorous attempts of less dominant suitors strenuously.

Anuran Oddities

Aside from having distinctly identifiable voices, frogs, toads, and treefrogs are among the oddest of all creatures. Who could resist a group that counts among its members amphibians with these characteristics?

A hairy frog: Well, not really. But during breeding season, the males of the West African ranid frog,

The filaments present on this male hairy frog indicate breeding readiness.

Trichobatrachus robustus (colloquially called the "hairy frog"), develop hairlike filaments of epidermis to increase the surface involved in oxygen transfer, so that the frogs can remain underwater near the egg clutches for longer periods.

A tailed frog: Or, how about a "tailed frog?" Well, there isn't really one of them either. But the so-called tailed frog of the Pacific northwest has an exterior copulatory organ that suggests a tail. Tailed frogs are the only frogs that effect internal fertilization of the eggs.

The largest frog: The West African Goliath frog, *Conraua (Gigantorana) goliath*, is the world's largest frog. This species attains a snout-to-vent length (SVL) of 11⅞ inches (30 cm) and a weight of more than 6½ pounds (2.9 kg).

The smallest frog: The world's tiniest frog is the Brazilian brachycephalid toad known scientifically as *Psyllophryne didactyla*. Its largest recorded SVL is about 3/8 of an inch (9.8 mm). This species has no common name. Only slightly larger is the Cuban leptodactylid, *Sminthillus limbatus*, which is adult at ⁷⁄₁₆ of an inch (11.5 mm).

A poisonous frog: The deadliest skin secretions are produced by the tiny arrow-poison frog, *Phyllobates terribilis*.

A poisonous toad: Marine or giant toads, *Bufo marinus*, produce a toxin in the shoulder (parotoid) glands that is so potent that it will debilitate or kill mammalian predators.

A lungless frog: The Titicaca frog, *Telmatobius culeus*, has no lungs. It respires through its baggy, highly vascularized skin.

The northernmost frog: Wood frogs, *Rana sylvatica,* range above the Arctic Circle in Alaska.

A turtle frog: The amazing turtle frog, *Myobatrachus gouldii*, of arid western Australia burrows deeply

A male tailed frog.

beneath the ground. Its egg clusters have been found nearly 4 feet (1.2 meters) deep in the earth. It is a species that undergoes direct development, having no free-swimming tadpole stage.

A "flying frog": Many tropical old-world and neotropical treefrogs are assisted in gliding jumps by extensive webbing between the fingers and toes.

Vibrations for communication: Besides the typical audible calls, the Puerto Rican white-lipped frog, *Leptodactylus albilabris*, produces vibrations by tapping its vocal sacs on the ground.

The very toxic Phyllobates bicolor *is often referred to as the bicolored arrow-poison frog. It is one of the three most toxic species of arrow-poison frogs.*

A male Darwin's frog.

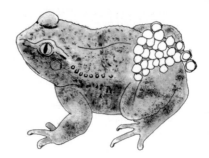

A male midwife toad carries strands of eggs around his waist.

Egg protection: The males of the Argentine (and Chilean) Darwin's frog, *Rhinoderma darwinii,* gather their soon-to-hatch eggs into their mouth. The eggs are then moved into the proportionately extensive vocal sac, where the tadpoles hatch, grow, and undergo metamorphosis. Finally, the youngsters emerge to begin life in the outside world.

In a variation on the above theme, the females of the (possibly extinct) Australian gastric-brooding frog, *Rheobatrachus silus*, and the still extant *R. vitellinus,* carry and "brood" their young in their stomach. Chemicals produced by the tadpoles inhibit the production of the female's digestive enzymes. The young are forcibly disgorged following metamorphosis!

A female marsupial treefrog releases her tadpoles into the water.

In yet another variation, the females of the neotropical marsupial treefrog, *Gastrotheca* sp., carry the fertilized eggs in a dorsal brood-pouch for a period of weeks. Once hatched, the tadpoles are released into quiet water to complete their development.

The egg strands of the European midwife toad, *Alytes obstetricians*, are wound around the waist of the male. Keeping the eggs moist by occasional immersions, he carries them until hatching time, when he deposits them in the water. (Other frog species carry the eggs or young in sacs on the groin, imbedded in the back, or merely adhering to the back, or even give birth to live offspring.)

Amphibian Names

Unlike the birds, animals, trees, and even people familiar to you, all of which have well-known common names, many amphibians and reptiles either have none or have names that vary from one area to another.

Many of the common names used for amphibians in pet shops or on dealers' lists are little more than marketing tools. Additionally, they may differ dramatically from shop to shop or dealer to dealer. Conversely, each species and subspecies of amphibian can have only one scientific name, and it does not vary, no matter where

A (Tentative) Family Tree

With vast fields of newly accumulated data at their fingertips, systematists are currently redetermining the relationships and taxonomy of frogs. As might be expected, the data is assessed differently by different researchers. We present here the anuran classifications suggested in 1985 by Darrel Frost (as amended by William E. Duellman in 1986).

Order Anura

Suborder Archaeobatrachia
  Family Leiopelmatidae
      Discoglossidae
  Family Paleobatrachidae
      (extinct)
      Pipidae
      Rhinophrynidae
  Family Pelobatidae
  Subfamily Eopelobatinae
      (extinct)
      Megophryinae
      Pelobatinae
  Family Pelodytidae

Suborder Neobatrachia
  Family Myobatrachidae
  Subfamily Limnodynastinae
      Myobatrachinae
  Family Heleophrynidae
  Family Sooglossidae

Family Leptodactylidae
Subfamily Ceratophryinae
      Telmatobiinae
      Hylodinae
      Leptodactylinae
Family Bufonidae
Family Brachycephalidae
Family Rhinodermatidae
Family Pseudidae
Family Hylidae
Subfamily Pelodryadinae
      Phyllomedusinae
      Hemiphractinae
      Hylinae
Family Centrolenidae
Family Dendrobatidae
Family Ranidae
Subfamily Arthroleptinae
      Astylosterninae
      Hemisinae
      Mantellinae
      Petropedetinae
      Raninae
Family Hyperoliidae
Family Rhacophoridae
Family Microhylidae
Subfamily Scaphiophryninae
      Dyscophinae
      Cophylinae
      Asterophryinae
      Genophryninae
      Breviciptinae
      Melanobatrachinae
      Phrynomerinae
      Microhylinae

---

you acquire your specimen. For instance, the Australian treefrog, *Litoria caerulea*, may be called White's treefrog, Australian green treefrog, Australian giant green treefrog, dumpy treefrog, or pudgy treefrog—but it can only be called *Litoria caerulea* when spoken of in scientific terms. We strongly suggest that you learn and use the scientific names of your creatures. Although these names may look and sound difficult at first, you will find that they are actually quite simple; and knowing them will help you immensely in the long run.

What Is Happening to the Frogs?

The frogs, toads, and treefrogs of the world are proving to be important *indicator* species. An indicator species is one that tells us a problem exists—be it with the environment or some other facet necessary for life.

Presently the populations of many of the frogs, toads, and treefrogs of

Without geographical data, many species in the genus Leptodactylus *are difficult to identify.* L. nigriventris *is a quietly colored but active Ecuadorian species of moderate size.*

the world are diminishing, or even disappearing, at alarming speed.

In a few short years Australia's gastric-brooding frog and Costa Rica's golden toad apparently have become extinct. Populations of the high-altitude neotropical harlequin frog are reduced. The Tarahumara frog no longer exists in its canyon strongholds in Arizona (it can still be found in northern Sonora, Mexico). All species and subspecies of the red-legged and yellow-legged frogs of our Pacific

The neotropical marsupial frog, Gastrotheca marsupiatum, *is a specialized hylid. Females carry the eggs in a pouch on their back.*

states are seriously diminished. Wyoming toads are teetering on the verge of extinction. Northern leopard frogs are becoming uncommon across much of their range.

What is causing these problems? Is it acid rain? Is it reduced ozone? How about pesticides . . . or airborne industrial pollution? Could it be ground waters polluted by factory runoffs? Perhaps it is a cumulative problem, involving all the above factors and more. Whatever it is, we need to isolate and correct the causes of these population reductions.

As amphibian populations become measurably reduced, remnant populations are being protected by laws that seem to change almost daily. To learn about all facets of the problems, we strongly recommend that you read *Tracking the Vanishing Frogs—An Ecological Mystery*, by Kathryn Phillips. This excellent book explains many of the problems that are increasing in magnitude with each passing day.

Laws

Frogs, toads, and treefrogs are increasingly protected by conservation laws. The laws of each state may differ widely in content or application. Before you collect the eggs, tadpoles, or adults of any native species of frog, toad, or treefrog (any wildlife or plants, for that matter), we urge that you check the laws of your state game and fisheries commissions and of the U.S. Department of the Interior. Penalties for breach of the laws (which can apply not only to collection, but to transportation, possession without permit, and sale or purchase of various species) can be severe. Ignorance is no excuse, nor is ignorance a worthy defense for a responsible hobbyist.

Unless they are headed for a true breeding facility, we believe that removal of additional specimens from the wild should be discouraged.

Frog Watching and Photographing

Everything about frog watching—and frog watchers—is diametrically opposed to bird watching—and bird watchers.

Bird watchers (with the exception of owl specialists) hope for a nice sunshiny day to head into the field with binoculars, tapes, field guide, and the like, all easily accessible and equally easy to assemble, read, and assimilate in the brilliant daylight. Frog watchers, on the other hand, hope for early darkness and cloudy nights. For some species, we might even hope for a torrential downpour (but a soft rain *might* suffice to make us smile). On moonless nights, we sally forth in darkness, burdened down with headlamps, flashlights, extra bulbs and batteries, tapes, and field guides. (Generally, we don't carry binoculars). Instead of flowering meadows, we head for swamps, marshes, woodland ponds, and seepages. There, we slog about, tracking down the snores, grunts, trills, and peeps of the nocturnal creatures we so enjoy. By the time we leave the swamps our waders (if we were smart enough to wear them) usually are filled with water that rushed in when we knelt in hopes of sighting a tiny anuran so camouflaged by body stripes that it looks more like the dead emergent grasses than a frog.

Although birds of some sort usually are present year round, frogs, toads, and treefrogs are much more seasonal. Over much of North America, we see most during the prehibernation time in November, and then nothing until the warming and lengthening days of spring have set in and induced amphibian emergence. By that time we are more than ready to trudge back to the field, plodding under the burden of all the paraphernalia we think we might need.

The calls of the frogs, toads, and treefrogs are as different as those of birds. Most of us know the strident sound of spring peepers, heard over much of the eastern half of our nation. These birdlike calls are voiced with a rising, quizzical inflection at the end. But to hear these minute frogs and to see them are entirely different things. If you are skeptical, become a frog-watcher—and you will be enchanted by the variety of the calls.

How do you start such a hobby? First, to learn the calls of the creatures you hope to see, you can attend night-time walks with a qualified naturalist (many nature centers and science museums offer such field trips) or buy a record or tape on which the calls are recorded and identified. We suggest that you do both. While learning to identify the voices of anurans, learn their habits as well. Some frogs call only from vernal pools, others from deep permanent fresh-water lakes, still others from river-swamps. Next learn the whereabouts of these various habitats. Then your new hobby is easy to pursue.

But do be aware that frog watching often leads to frog photographing, and if you thought you were heavily laden before . . .

HOW-TO:
Photographing Frogs, Toads, and Treefrogs

Photographing amphibians can be a demanding but fulfilling pursuit. It is one that we enjoy immensely. Many hobbyists see photography as the best method of documenting captive or wild behavior patterns. It is a way of "keeping" an anuran with no work—once the photograph has been made. Capturing an anuran—even a relatively inactive specimen—on film often requires that stealth and field knowledge be combined with the discipline of photography. As you progress, each photo will help you see how to improve the next. Getting started is easy.

The equipment required will depend upon a number of variables. Among these are whether you will be taking both long-distance field photos and staged close-ups. Of course, photographing captive or staged frogs, toads, and treefrogs is infinitely easier than pursuing and photographing free-ranging ones, but not nearly so satisfying.

Basic Equipment

A sturdy 35 mm camera body with interchangeable lenses is a good choice. You don't need a brand-new camera body and lenses; we've used quality second-hand equipment for many of our photographic ventures. You do need a photo supply dealer who can accurately advise you about the condition of the equipment you're buying, and who can tell you about some features of that particular lens or body (usually, second-hand camera equipment does not come with manuals).

Lenses: The lenses we use include:
• 28 mm wide angle for habitat photos
• 50 mm standard for habitat photos
• 100 mm macro for close-ups (suitable for almost every purpose)
• 75–205 mm zoom lens for variable field work
• 400 mm fixed-focal-length telephoto lens for field work
• 120–600 mm zoom lens for distant but variable field work

Strobes: A series of dedicated strobes. (A dedicated strobe interfaces with the camera f-stop setting to furnish appropriate light levels.)

Lens adapter: a ×1.25 power magnifier or a ×2 doubler.

Film: ISO 50 slide film is slower and less "grainy" than higher-speed films. This slower film will yield the best results, but it also requires a bright day or electronic flashes to compensate for the slow speed. The higher the ISO, the less light you will need to photograph, but the "grainier" your pictures will be. If you are taking pictures with the hope of having them published, use ISO 50 slide film. If you are taking them merely for your own enjoyment, use either slide or print film, as you prefer.

Tripod: A sturdy tripod (an absolute necessity for the telephoto lenses) will hold your camera steady while you squeeze off that "once in a lifetime" shot. Camera equipment is heavy, especially if you are out in the field and have slogged through hip-deep water and scaled a couple of hillsides. (The equipment is heavy even if you're indoors.)

Camera body: After having a camera body malfunction on occasion, we now always have at least one spare body available.

A highly effective stage can be made from readily available material. In this case black velvet is draped over a cut-off trash can, which is bolted to a Lazy Susan base.

Some Photographic Hints

For staged photography, create a small natural setting by placing rocks, mosses, leaves, or bark—whichever is most appropriate for the species you're photographing—on a stage. We use a small lazy Susan as a stage. This enables us to rotate the stage (with the animal on it), for different photographic angles. This works, providing you move *very slowly* in all your actions, including rotating the stage. If you have no lazy Susan, arrange the scenery on a table top or a tree stump, put the anuran in place, focus, and shoot. Having a photo assistant to help pose or catch the leaping frog will help. We use the top half of a round trash can for the backing of our stage. We first cut it to size then firmly bolt it in place. Black velvet clipped into place around the inside surface of the can makes a good background. The result is an easily moved, eminently serviceable stage.

Field photography can be considerably more trying than staged photography. To accomplish the former successfully, it is almost mandatory that you have an assistant.

Approaching a nocturnal anuran with a camera while keeping the creature in a flashlight beam can be truly exasperating. Generally, if you move very slowly the animal will remain in place long enough to permit a

Field photography is always easier if you have the help of a friend.

few shots. You or your partner will need to move quickly to capture the specimen if it moves, replace it where you wish to photograph it, then move slowly to refocus and shoot.

If you're trying field photography, approach the animal slowly and obliquely. Avoid eye contact. If the amphibian notices you (as it almost certainly will), freeze for a moment, then begin moving again. Eventually, if you are lucky, you will be close enough to get the field shot you wanted.

When done, retrace your steps carefully, disturbing as little habitat as possible, and leaving nothing behind—nothing, that is, except your footprints and the specimen that you just photographed successfully.

Caging Techniques

Understanding Microenvironments

To understand the caging needs of the anurans, it is necessary to know a little about the creatures themselves and the natural microenvironment to which each is adapted.

What do we mean by microenvironment? Let's take a Sonoran green toad as an example.

Sonoran green toads, *Bufo retiformis*, are beautiful little creatures indigenous to the Sonoran Desert of Arizona and northern Mexico. Now, how would you maintain a Sonoran green toad successfully in captivity?

Well—the Sonoran Desert *is* a desert, right? And, by definition, a desert is hot and dry—right? So, to

The Sonoran green toad, Bufo retiformis, *is the most colorful toad of the USA. This species occurs in southcentral Arizona and adjacent Mexico.*

keep a Sonoran green toad successfully, you keep it hot and dry—right?

If you answered the last three questions "yes," "yes," and "yes" you were right, partially right, and completely wrong.

Although most deserts are both hot and dry at some point in every calendar year, not all deserts are created equal in these respects. In fact, a Sonoran green toad cannot long survive the heat and drought of the open desert. If you keep your toad hot and dry, you'll kill it, pure and simple!

You see, within any given environment there are microenvironments (or microhabitats), and each of these smaller subdivisions provides protection and nurture to its own coterie of specifically adapted creatures. The shade of a desert bush on a hot day provides life-giving coolness, the subsurface sand offers another habitat, while the barely moist environs of the rare desert stream or pond offer yet another microenvironment. And so it goes—the desert sand, the rocky bottom of an ephemeral stream, the shade and cool of a canyon—each offers something different to different creatures. And some of those creatures are adapted to survive nowhere else.

The Sonoran green toad inhabits areas of slight to moderate moisture found near desert oases, streams, and ponds. In such habitats it can thrive and multiply. During the desert monsoons that stimulate breeding activities for this and other arid-land amphibians, it may even wander for short distances into the surrounding desert—but not so far that it can't quickly and easily return to the (moderately) less hostile environs to which it is best adapted. During extremely dry or cold weather, the Sonoran green toad buries itself well below the surface of the ground. The return of warmth and dampness induces it upward. It may emerge to forage when the ground cools after nightfall. Once the monsoons have set in, refreshing streams and filling shrunken desert waterholes, the little toads queue up evenings and voice their bleating trills during the short but busy breeding season. Following this period of activity, if moist or even humid weather lingers, or while standing or subsurface water remains available in desert depressions, the toads will remain active.

However, when all again becomes dry and sere, the green toads seek refuge beneath the sands, where they await additional moisture before reemerging.

What did all of that tell us?

1. Toads—even desert toads—do not like complete dryness.

2. Toads, including desert toads, are active after nightfall when relative humidity is higher and the chance of desiccation is reduced.

3. The fact that an animal is found in a desert doesn't necessarily mean that it is adapted to absolute aridity; in fact, most animals aren't.

4. It is mandatory that you know the specific needs of your animal; that you not assume that a desert is a desert is a desert and that any creature occurring within its confines is adapted to absolute drought. Learn the needs of your creatures, then adapt your cages accordingly.

Indoor Caging

The Simplest of the Simple

Some folks prefer the simple approach to terrarium making and keeping. Happily for them, some frogs,

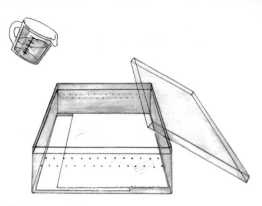

Plastic sweater boxes can serve as a simple terrarium for many hardy anurans.

toads, and treefrogs will thrive in the simplest of containers.

Damp paper towels: Horned, Budgett's, and Chacoan burrowing frogs, as well as most toads, will thrive in a setup as simple as a plastic sweater or blanket box either with dampened paper towels covering the entire bottom or tilted slightly with a little clean water in the low end. To clean, remove the toweling, scrub the box, and replace the toweling; or empty the water, scrub the box, and replace the water. Dechlorinate/dechloramine the fresh water as necessary,

A very basic terrarium for White's and other treefrogs can be made from an aquarium, paper towels, a water dish, and a mounted limb.

using products for this purpose that are available at pet and aquarium stores.

Dampened towels plus: White's (and other quiet) treefrog species may be kept in suitably sized 10 to 50 gallons (approximately 35–200 L) terrariums with dampened paper towels, kraft paper, or even dampened newsprint on the bottom. The necessary water is supplied in a readily removed and cleaned shallow dish (such as an ashtray), and a perching limb (piece of sterilized driftwood or gnarled manzanita branch) is provided. The paper substrate must be removed and replaced when soiled, the water bowl should be scrubbed and fresh water provided every second or third day (more frequently if the water is dirtied), and the glass panes cleaned once or twice a week. We also sterilize and thoroughly rinse the perch about twice a month.

Water only: Even aquatic species can be maintained in a very plain setup with no substrate, cage furnishings, filtration, or other amenities (suitable warmth is imperative, though). The water must be changed more frequently when filtration is not provided. (In the long run this very basic design makes more work than the full setup described below.)

There are, of course, other ways to make terrariums—some of them far, far more intricate and sophisticated.

Aquatic Species

Of the many kinds of frogs and toads now available to hobbyists, only a handful of species are entirely aquatic. Those you are most apt to find are the dwarf underwater and clawed frogs and the fire-bellied and Surinam toads. Of course, tadpoles of most species will also thrive in an aquarium until metamorphosis begins. Then specialized care is necessary (see page 34).

Your aquatic frogs' and toads' tank should be set up and maintained in precisely the same manner as an aquarium for fish. Water quality, including the removal of chlorine and chloramine, is *very* important. Keep in mind the tremendous weight of an aquarium filled with water and gravel substrate. Be sure to use an aquarium stand or some other very sturdy, level surface. If your tank is not adequately supported all around the bottom frame, the weight and pressure of the water and gravel will break panels of glass. Proper bottom support of "show" or "high" tanks is especially critical.

The final appearance of your tank setup will probably be dictated by the kinds of frogs and toads you intend to keep.

The dwarf underwater frogs: These tiny creatures are so fond of a lushly planted aquarium that we can seldom resist the desire to provide one. Additionally, their minuscule size makes it entirely possible to keep a half dozen in something as small as a 5-gallon (approximately 20 L) tank—though larger is preferable, of course.

We prefer substrates of at least 2 inches (5 cm) of smooth, pea-sized river gravel, intricate arrangements of submerged driftwood and rocks, and a profusion of live aquatic plants. When we are done with the arrangement, you can usually see the frogs only when they choose to be seen.

Heating for these tiny frogs can be provided by either a standard or a submersible aquarium heater. Several types of filtration devices are available. Standard foam cartridge corner filters (which operate from an equally standard vibrator pump) are efficient, as are outside filters. However, our current favorite is a foam cartridge to which a submersible power head is attached. These models seem highly efficient and very adaptable, and they provide both mechanical and biological filtration.

Adequate and proper lighting is essential when you grow live plants in your aquarium. We usually utilize at least two full-length fluorescent plant-grow bulbs (more if the aquarium is in a dark area of the house) over each aquarium setup.

The fire-bellied toads: These small, pretty toads also do very well in an aquarium setup. However, since they are less thoroughly aquatic than the underwater frogs, a haulout area must be provided. We use floating corkbark, driftwood, and mats of growing, floating aquarium plants. The fire-bellies are very adept at clambering aboard any of these "islands" when choosing to leave the water.

The clawed frogs and Surinam toads: Much larger than either species described above, these anurans will quickly rearrange and uproot most cage furniture and plantings. We merely use an inch or two (2.5–5 cm) of pea-sized gravel and driftwood pieces that will not break the aquarium glass if brought sharply into contact by the maneuverings and kickings of the frogs. Keep the glass breakage factor in mind if using rocks for decoration. They must either be so large that frogs can't move them; or if small, anchored with silicone aquarium sealant to the bottom or back of the tank. Even a small rock, when shoved by powerful hindlegs, can have a devastating effect on panels of aquarium glass.

The glass tubes of aquarium heaters are also very prone to breakage when shoved about by the larger frogs. Anchor the heaters very securely and check the anchors frequently. If a heater is broken, unplug it *before* putting your hands or any other implement in the water.

If you keep clawed or dwarf underwater frogs or Surinam toads, a haulout area is not necessary.

Semiaquatic Species

It is somewhat more difficult to maintain "absolute" cleanliness in a semiaquatic terrarium than in a wholly aquatic setup. In compensation, the beauty that can be created in a semiaquatic arrangement will help make the extra effort worthwhile. There are several rather simple and effective ways to construct semiaquatic enclosures.

Using charcoal: In all semiaquatic and woodland/forest terrariums a base layer of activated charcoal may be used under the land area to remove contaminants. When we do use this, we place a piece of air-conditioner filter material over the charcoal to keep the gravel from becoming mixed in. There was a time when we would not construct a terrarium without the charcoal. Now, we may or may not use it. We have found virtually no difference in serviceability.

River rock: Sufficient pea-sized river rock should be used to design the desired bottom contour. We generally build somewhat more than half of the bottom up to a depth of about 5 inches (12.7 cm). This will be the land section of the tank. The remaining section, which will hold the water, has a gravel covering only a half inch (12.7 mm) or so in depth. The gravel, of course, slopes gently from one section to the other; the pea-sized pieces stay pretty much in place.

Atop the built-up land area we then place an inch (2.5 cm) or so of sterilized topsoil; atop the soil we lay several stems of a vining pothos or philodendron. These quickly root from the leaf nodes, and if lighting is adequate, will soon form a jungle. Mossy logs and stones can be easily and artistically incorporated into the design. If we choose to add variety to the plant life, we sink other moisture-tolerant species (fitonia, maranta, etc.) right in their pots to pot-rim in the gravel and soil. We then add water to a depth of about 2 inches (5 cm).

The cleaning of a semiaquatic terrarium such as this is not at all difficult. To flush the land area, we simply pour water onto it. As the water percolates through the gravel, it will carry with it a little topsoil and many of the impurities present. Then after moving a little of the gravel to expose the glass bottom in a corner of the tank, we siphon the water from the terrarium. We often run from 5 to 10 gallons (about 20–40 L) of water through in this manner before finally adding the water that will remain. The water used, both for the cleaning process and for the final refilling, must have had the chlorine and chloramines removed. Amphibians are nearly as sensitive as fish to these additives.

Many people dislike this method of creating a semiaquatic terrarium because the flushing and cleaning of the land area always carries into the water some soil or discoloration. We consider that a normal, hence not unattractive, feature of this style of terrarium.

"Solid" land: The next style of construction allows you to avoid most of the discoloration problem. Here the land section is divided from the water section by a sloped piece of fitted glass siliconed securely in place with the top tilted toward the land section. The upper side of the sloped glass should be thinly coated with silicone sealant over which a fine dusting of sand is strewn before the sealant dries. That will give the anuran inhabitants a toehold on what would otherwise be a dangerously slippery surface.

The land section is constructed as described earlier—that is, a thick basal layer of pea-sized gravel covered with a layer of potting soil. Additional water cleanliness can be ensured by placing a layer of sphagnum moss atop the potting soil.

The sealed glass partitioning has two advantages: the water level can be any depth desired and, since gravel depths can be reduced in the water area, overall terrarium weight can be lessened.

The land area can be lavishly or sparsely planted. We use such terrarium-compatible plants as fitonia, maranta, pothos, and vining philodendrons. Arboreal bromeliads provide many arrow-poison frogs with their preferred sites for egg deposition. Saggiteria and other hardy emergents can be grown in the aquatic end. Driftwood, mossy logs, mossy rocks, or similar decorations that provide additional beauty can be used in either the water or the land area, as desired or suited.

Mostly land: This type of semi-aquatic tank is the easiest of all. The water is contained in a suitably sized plastic dish sunk to its rim in an extensive land section. Cleaning is accomplished by merely lifting the water dish out, sterilizing and refilling it, and replacing it in the tank. The land section is constructed as outlined earlier in this account.

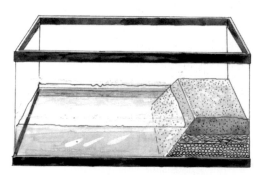

The land area of a semi-aquatic terrarium can be built behind a piece of slanted glass held in place with aquarium sealant.

Woodland Species

Woodland or rainforest terrariums will suit many frogs perfectly. Among these are the various mantellas and arrow-poison frogs. Except for one or two small, shallow water dishes, all else is moss-covered land that is profusely planted with woodland or rain-forest vegetation.

With the current availability of submersible power heads, riverine and waterfall woodland tanks may be easily designed. There are even terrariums available with tough plastic inserts that allow you to design and plant a mossy woodland stream bank/seepage area.

Variations on a theme: The intricacy of the terrarium will be limited only by imagination and available funds. For arboreal frog species, the height of the terrarium merits as much consideration as the floor space. If you are housing terrestrial anurans, the height of the cage is far less important.

Horizontal or vertical: A glass terrarium may be oriented in the standard ("top-up") position for terrestrial frog species, or in an upright position for arboreal species. A suitable top (or front, as the case may be) must be provided. With the standard orientation this poses no problem. With the upright orientation, however, devising an escape-proof front becomes more difficult. This task may be approached from two angles. First, if not *too* heavy, a glass front may be cut and held in position with a hinge of silicone aquarium sealant. A hook and hasp may be similarly attached on the opposite side. We have found that if the edge of the glass door rests flush against the table or stand top (or the inside glass of the aquarium) the sealant hinge receives much less stress. A plexiglass rectangle can be substituted for glass, but plexiglass scratches very easily. However, if the door does become too scratched for easy viewing of the cage occupants, it is a simple matter to replace it.

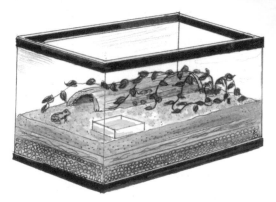

A woodland terrarium should contain vining plants, hiding areas, and a water dish.

The second method is to locate your terrarium an inch or two (2.5–5 cm) off the flat surface on blocks or legs. A tightly fitting framed front can then be slipped over the open side. (If the front is divided in half, it will be easier to restrain nervous specimens.)

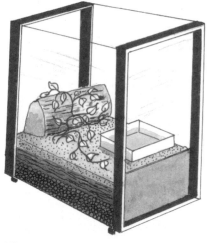

When a vertically oriented terrarium is placed on short legs, glass or screening may be used to cover the open side.

Outdoor Caging

Construction Tips

Generally, caging used in an outdoors setting is made from wood and wire. This prevents the heat build-up that occurs in glass terrariums and permits the anurans to take limited amounts of unfiltered sun. When building large wood and wire terrariums/cages, it is a good idea to incorporate casters into their design so that they may be easily moved about. In warm climates, where many frogs, toads, and treefrogs can remain outdoors for most or all of the year, we have successfully used large "step-in" caging for many arboreal species. Those that we use have cage dimensions (height/length, width) of 66 inches × 48 inches × 30 inches (168 cm × 122 cm × 16 cm). The frames are made of 2 × 2 lumber, the base from ¾ inch marine plywood. The wire is ⅛ inch mesh hardware cloth. (The small mesh

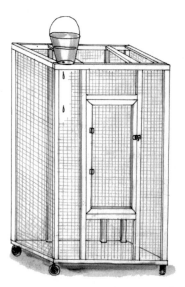

Outdoor cages of wood and wire construction can be tailored to meet most needs. Besides a drip bucket, an overhead lamp could be added if necessary.

of the wire ensures that all but the smallest feed crickets will remain within the cage.) Casters raise the overall height to 71 inches (180 cm), which allows the cages to be rolled indoors (through sliding patio doors or a single doorway opening), or even from room to room, as needed if the weather turns too cool. If left outdoors during cool weather, the cages are wrapped in clear 4 mil vinyl or polyethylene sheeting. This is stapled in place on three sides, but it can be rolled up and put out of the way or removed from the top and south (door) side if desired. A light in a reflector hood is used when necessary. To assure the comfort of the amphibians, the vinyl—except for the removable front and top—can (and probably should) remain in place throughout the winter months. In such setups, many treefrogs will bask for hours on sunny uprights of the frame or on the horizontals of the door frame.

Setting up the Large Cage

The bottom can be left bare. Alternatively, a low frame that will retain a clean sand substrate can be installed. While we do use sand on the bottoms of our cages, we merely pile it high in the cage center and let it seek its own level (including being washed out during storms). We also utilize hardy potted plants (cycads or ficus) within the cages. These provide decoration, visual barriers, and sites for egg deposition by the foam-nest treefrog species. Most species soon feel secure enough in these setups to breed naturally, with no artificial inducements whatever.

Cage Furnishings

Cage furnishings for frogs, toads, and treefrogs are usually chosen because they are attractive. Rock formations and caves will provide both beauty and a hiding area for your anurans. Sturdy-leaved plants and limbs

Cage furniture, in this case a rock formation, limb, sturdy plant, and cactus skeleton, should be aesthetically pleasing, functional, and easily sterilized.

will provide perches and visual barriers as well as add beauty to the terrarium.

If multilayered rock formations or caves are used, the rocks should be held in place (and together) with a nontoxic adhesive. Latex or silicone aquarium sealant is quite satisfactory for this purpose. If even a single flat rock is placed on the surface of the sand, you need to make sure that it cannot shift and injure your frogs should they burrow beneath it. Either natural rocks or decorative glass-rocks can be used.

Sand-blasted manzanita, grape, and other gnarled woods are often available at pet shops or from the wild. These provide perches and visual barriers for terrarium inhabitants.

Corkbark comes in many shapes and sizes. It is available in small tubes into which shy specimens can retire. In curved lengths, cork can provide lightweight caves when laid atop the terrarium's substrate.

Our tip: The curved cedar hideboxes often seen in pet shops are not satisfactory for use with amphibians. Cedar contains natural ingredients that are detrimental—even dangerous—to the health of many amphibian species.

Plants of many types are readily available and serve many purposes in a terrarium. Stiff-leafed types such as sanseverias or aloes make good perches and visual barriers. Additionally, some tailless amphibians like to deposit their eggs on the leaves of stiff-leafed plants. Unfortunately, these are succulent plants that do not thrive under the moist conditions required by many frogs, toads, and treefrogs.

Terrarium Cleanliness

No matter what type of caging you provide, the need for cleanliness in any amphibian caging facility cannot be overemphasized. All amphibians have permeable skins through which both moisture and impurities are absorbed. The lack of absolute cleanliness will most assuredly transmit potentially lethal pathogens to your frogs, toads, or treefrogs.

The substrate should be changed or flushed as often as necessary. The number and sizes of specimens in the terrarium will be instrumental in dictating cleaning or changing regimens. The perches should be scraped and washed as necessary, and all hard surfaces, such as rocks and glass, cleaned and sterilized. Water, whether in bowls or daily mists, must be fresh and clean.

If you are using a sand, gravel, or pebble substrate, it can be sterilized, dried, and reused. Dirty wood chips or mulch should be discarded and replaced with new ones. To sterilize sand, perches, twigs, rocks, cork bark, cholla skeletons and the terrarium itself, use a diluted solution of either Ro-Cal or chlorine bleach. After cleaning and sterilizing the items, be sure all are thoroughly rinsed with clean, fresh water.

Terrarium cleanliness will do much to ensure the long-term health of your frogs, toads, and treefrogs. Regular cleaning will help prevent the spread of both diseases and endoparasites. The cleaning should be a prominent part of your husbandry regimen.

Caution: Do not use pine oils or other phenol-based disinfectants for cleaning reptile and amphibian cages. Phenols are not tolerated well by herps. Even lingering odors can be deleterious.

Lighting and Heating

Terrarium lights can be used not only for illuminating a cage, but also as a reliable and easily controlled heat source during cold weather. Rather inexpensive in-line thermostats or rheostats can be installed by electricians. Plug-in timers are readily available at hardware stores.

If additional warmth is needed, heating pads, heat-tapes, and undertank heaters are all readily available. Do not use of hot rocks for amphibians.

Always provide a thermal gradient (warm to cool) within any terrarium.

Do not use pine oils or other phenol-based cleaners in amphibian cages.

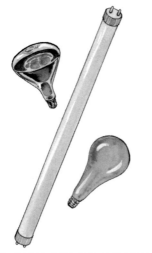

Floodlamps, full-spectrum fluorescent tubes, and plant grow bulbs are readily available forms of illumination. You must always remember that the heat produced by incandescent bulbs can quicky kill a captive amphibian.

Avoiding Electrical Accidents

It is important to use caution when handling electrical equipment and wiring, which are particularly hazardous when used in connection with water. Always observe the following safeguards carefully:

• Before using any of the electrical equipment described in this book, check to be sure that it carries the UL symbol.

• Keep all lamps away from water or spray.

• Before using any equipment in water, check the label to make sure it is suitable for underwater use.

• Disconnect the main electrical plug before you begin any work in a water terrarium or touch any equipment.

• Be sure that the electric current you use passes through a central fuse box or circuit-breaker system. Such a system should be installed only by a licensed electrician.

Full Spectrum Lighting

Ultraviolet light (UV): Theories of amphibians' exact UV requirements remain conjectural. Diurnal species of frogs, toads, and treefrogs obviously would be subjected to more UV in their natural surroundings than nocturnal species. Even diurnal deep-forest dwellers would receive reflected UV. Most of the readily available incandescent light bulbs provide no UV; they serve only to illuminate and supply auxiliary warmth. A new generation of "full-spectrum" incandescent bulbs may eventually provide appropriate UV.

Full-spectrum fluorescent bulbs do provide some UV, but prove beneficial only when located a foot or so (about 30 cm) away from the animals. Their UV emissions are weak.

With reptiles, it is known that UV-A promotes natural behavior and UV-B promotes the synthesizing of vitamin D_3 and the absorption of calcium.

Sunlight: Unfiltered natural sunlight is the best provider of UV. If filtered through most glasses and plexi-glasses, most of the UV is removed from natural sunlight.

Caution: Do not place a glass terrarium in sunlight. Even in cold weather the glass can concentrate the heat, which might kill or disable your amphibians.

Wire-covered wood-frame cages are best suited to take advantage of natural sunlight in outdoor locations. Clear plastic can be stapled over three sides to reduce cool breezes or help concentrate warmth in cool weather. Again, when plastic is used, always watch to make sure temperatures do not become too hot in the cage. Caging setups such as these are ideal for White's and red-eyed treefrogs and similar species.

Water Dishes and Misting

Water dishes are not necessary for all frogs, toads, and treefrogs. This is especially true of species that dwell in humid terrariums (check individual species accounts for specific suggestions). Persistently arboreal species will obtain sufficient moisture from the droplets on freshly misted leaves. Misting should be done daily. However, if a water receptacle is provided it must be kept *absolutely* clean.

Water dishes may be used but must be kept clean and fresh.

The Hydration Chamber

The uses and benefits of hydration chambers, long appreciated by zoos and other public institutions, are only now coming into general use by private herpetoculturists and hobbyists. Hydration chamber is merely a highfalutin' term for "rain chamber." But there is nothing highfalutin' about the chamber's value to the herpetoculturist. These receptacles can make the difference between life and death for dehydrated frogs, toads, and treefrogs, and perform vital functions in the reproductive cycling of these and other amphibians. It is usually during the evening rains of spring or the early rainy season

When misting terrarium specimens, direct the spray upwards, allowing the droplets to settle like those of a gentle rain.

that amphibians are stimulated to breed. A week or so of evening mistings in a hydration chamber will often have the same effect as natural rains.

Making your own: A hydration chamber can be constructed of wire mesh over a wood frame, or of an aquarium equipped with a circulating water pump and a screen or perforated plexiglass top. If you are fortunate enough to live in a benign climate where the cage can be placed outdoors, a mist nozzle can be attached to the end of a hose, affixed over the cage, and fresh water run through this for an hour or more a day. (If your community chlorinates the water supply, the mist nozzle technique can be detrimental to amphibians, all of which have permeable skins.)

If indoors, the cage can be placed on or inside a properly drained utility tub and the fresh water system used. It is imperative that the drain system be adequate and be kept free of debris if this system is used indoors. A secondary (backup) drain might do much to guarantee your peace of mind.

In self-contained systems, the circulation pump can force water from the tank itself through a small-diameter PVC pipe into which a series of lateral holes has been drilled. Alternatively, the water can be brought up to the top of the tank and allowed to drip through the screen or perforated plexiglass. It is essential that the water in self-contained systems be kept immaculately clean.

Advantages of a chamber: The use of a hydration unit can do much to help moisture-starved herptiles recuperate. Those that will most benefit from such a structure are the rain-forest species that are freighted long distances to the pet markets of America, Asia, Europe, and other continents. The various treefrogs, flying frogs, and other thin-bodied frogs are among the prime candidates for hydration-chamber treatment.

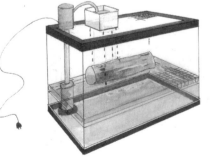

When used prudently the "rainfall" from a simple hydration chamber will be beneficial to amphibians.

Diets

When adult, all frogs, toads, and treefrogs are either carnivores or insectivores. Some larger species regularly prey on small mammals and birds. Others eat smaller frogs, or fish, or reptiles. But in captivity, most can be accustomed to feed on insects or rodents that are easily available to us. Still, it will behoove you to learn your frog's natural dietary habits, because some specialized species may refuse all else. The first step in learning the dietary needs of a species is to accurately identify it. The remaining tasks will fall quickly into place. You may need to be innovative to persuade your frog, toad, or treefrog to feed. If it has been deprived of food for a lengthy period by the collector or wholesaler, it may require considerable prodding to start feeding again. It will be your responsibility to offer fresh food in such secure and calming surroundings that your specimen cannot resist the temptation. Once it has begun feeding again, it probably will continue to do so; and it may even expand its horizons to include a food type quite different from that natural to it.

Insects

So your frogs like insects—what could be easier? At first, finding a few crickets, houseflies, or grasshoppers seems simple. After a week or two of daily searches for insects, reality sets in: Buying feed insects is much easier than hunting them down.

But there's more to feeding your frogs insects than tossing a few crickets into the cage. You need to feed the insects well before you offer them to your amphibians. Caring properly for feed insects is an important aspect of successful herpetological husbandry. A poorly fed or otherwise unhealthy insect offers little but bulk to a reptile or an amphibian. You may watch your frogs or toads eat feed insects every day, yet if the insects are not healthy, your amphibians may be slowly starving or developing a malady such as metabolic bone disease. Maintaining feed insects in top-notch health should be a main concern of any herpetoculturist.

Feeding food insects: "Gut-loading" means feeding your insects an abundance of highly nutritious foods immediately before they are offered as food to your specimens. Calcium, vitamin D_3, fresh fruit and vegetables, fresh alfalfa and/or bean sprouts, honey, and vitamin/mineral-enhanced (chick) laying mash are only a few of the foods suitable for gut-loading insects. You might also consider a prepared gut-loading diet that recently reached the marketplace. Insects quickly lose much of their food value if not continually fed an abundance of highly nourishing foodstuffs. Most insects eat continually, so much benefit accrues to your amphibians if you supply the insects with the highest-quality diet possible.

Except for "field plankton," all feed insects, even houseflies, are commercially available. You may prefer to avail yourself regularly of the various commercial sources. Certainly this is less time-consuming than breeding your own insects. However, by breeding your own you can assure that the

In many areas, insects can be easily gathered with a sweep net.

best possible diet is available to the insects. If you decide to procure the insects commercially, you should feed them the best diet possible as soon as soon as possible.

Field plankton: Insects straight "from the wild" are already well-fed. Because they have been able to choose their diet, their nutritive value is high. Field plankton, probably the best diet you can offer your insectivorous amphibians, is a mixture of the various insects and arachnids that can be field-collected in any given location. To gather them, simply sweep a suitably meshed field net back and forth through tall grasses or low shrubs in an area you known to be chemical-free.

Having fed naturally on natural, native foods, these insects are probably in prime condition. Immediately after collection feed them to your frogs, toads, or treefrogs. The full guts of these healthy insects will be of high nutritive value to the amphibians.

Our tip: Be sure to place a container of insect food in your terrarium when you provide insects for your frogs and toads. Insects are opportunistic feeders and have been known to prey upon anurans.

Crickets

The gray cricket, *Acheta domesticus,* is now bred commercially both for fishing bait and for pet food. Other cricket species are readily collected in small numbers beneath debris in fields, meadows, and open woodlands. If available in suitable sizes, all species of crickets are ideal amphibian foods.

Where to get them: Gray crickets are now so inexpensive that few hobbyists breed them. If you need only a few, they can be purchased from local pet shops. If you use several hundred to several thousand crickets weekly, purchase them from wholesale pro-

Crickets should be healthy and "gut-loaded" before being offered to amphibians as food.

ducers that advertise in fishing or reptile magazines. You will find the prices are quite reasonable when crickets are purchased in multiples of 1,000.

Cricket care: Crickets fed on potatoes are fine for fishing, but you need to offer them a better diet if they are to benefit your amphibians. Potato-fed crickets cannot provide your anurans with the correct vitamin and mineral fare to prevent nutritional disorders. Feed your crickets a good, varied diet of your own making, or one of the nutritious formulated cricket foods now on the market. Among other foods, fresh carrots, potatoes, broccoli, oranges, squash, sprouts, and chick laying mash will be readily consumed. All foods offered your crickets should be sprinkled with calcium and vitamin D_3. Crickets will be cannibalistic if crowded or underfed. While crickets will get much of their moisture requirements from fruit and vegetables, they will also appreciate a water source. However, crickets will drown easily if they are just given a shallow water dish. Instead, place cotton balls, a sponge, or even pebbles in the dish. These will give the crickets sufficient purchase to climb back out if they happen to fall in.

Cricket housing: Keep crumpled newspapers, paper towel tubes, or other such hiding areas in the cricket's cage. We prefer the paper towel tubes because they can be lifted and the requisite number of crickets shaken from inside them into the cage or a transportation jar. This makes handling the fast-moving, agile insects easy. A tightly covered 20-gallon (75 L) long tank will temporarily house 1,000 crickets. A substrate of sawdust, soil, vermiculite, or other such medium should be present. This must be changed often to prevent excessive odor from the insects.

Breeding your own: If you choose to breed your own crickets, this is not difficult. Keep the temperature of the cricket cage between 76 and 86°F (24.5–30°C). Place a shallow dish of slightly moistened sand, vermiculite, or cotton balls on the floor of the cage. The material will be the laying medium, which must be kept very slightly moistened throughout the laying, incubation, and hatching processes. Adult crickets are easily sexed. Females have three "tubes" (the central one being the egg-depositing organ, or ovipositor) projecting from the rear of their bodies. Males lack the central ovipositor. The ovipositor is inserted into the laying medium and the eggs expelled. The eggs will hatch in eight to 20 days, the duration being determined by cricket species and tank temperature. Nutritious food should always be available to the baby crickets.

Uses for the hatchlings: Newly hatched crickets are ideal for arrow-poison frogs, mantellas, other small species, or the babies of most larger species. Pinhead-sized crickets may be the largest morsels some of the smallest frogs can handle.

Grasshoppers and Locusts

Grasshoppers and locusts (*Locusta* sp. and *Shistocerca* sp. in part) are widely used as reptile and amphibian foods in Europe and Asia, and are commercially available there. In the United States, you will have to breed them or collect them in the field. However, grasshoppers are fast, and it may take some time for you to build

In suitable sizes, non-noxious grasshoppers and locusts can be important feed items.

up your "netting" skills. You may wish to remove the large "hopping" legs before you place these insects in with your amphibians.

Our tip: In some southern areas large, slow grasshoppers called "lubbers" may be found. Many of them have a brightly colored (often black and yellow or red) nymphal stage that can be fatally toxic if eaten by your specimens. The tan and buff adults seem to be less toxic, but their use as food is not advisable.

Waxworms

The "waxworm" (*Galleria* sp.) is the larval stage of the wax moth, which frequently infests neglected beehives. Waxworms are available commercially from many sources. Frequently used as fish bait, they are available from tackle stores. Check the ads in any reptile and amphibian magazine for wholesale distributors. Some pet shops also carry waxworms.

Waxworm tips: If you buy wholesale quantities of waxworms, you will need to feed them. Chick laying mash, wheat germ, honey, and yeast mixed into a syrupy paste will serve adequately as a diet for these insects.

Giant Mealworms

Giant mealworms, *Zoophobas* sp., are the larvae of a South American beetle. They are rather new in the herpetocultural trade, and at present (1996), their ready availability is being threatened in the United States by the Department of Agriculture. This situation is unfortunate for reptile breeders, for *Zoophobas* have proven to be a great food source for many frogs, toads, and treefrogs. Although they are still available in some states and virtually all of Europe and Asia, it would seem prudent for American herpetoculturists to begin breeding their own.

Keeping your own: *Zoophobas* can be kept in quantity in shallow plastic trays containing an inch or so (about 2.5 cm) of sawdust. They can be fed a diet of chick starting mash, bran, leafy vegetables, and apples.

Breeding your own: To induce pupation, place one giant mealworm each in a series of empty film canisters or other similar small containers filled with sawdust, bran, or oats. Nestle the film containers together in a larger box to keep them together and in an upright position. You don't need lids because the larvae won't climb out. After a few days the worms will pupate, eventually metamorphosing into black beetles. The beetles can be placed in a plastic tub containing a sawdust substrate and old cracked

Giant mealworms can be metamorphosed individually in film canisters. Mealworms derive necessary moisture from pieces of fruit and vegetables.

limbs and twigs for egg laying. (The female beetles deposit their eggs in the crevices in the limbs.) The beetles and their larvae can be fed vegetables, fruits, oats, and bran. Giant mealworms will obtain all of their moisture requirements from the fresh vegetables and fruit.

Multiple colonies: You can keep several colonies to ensure that you have all sizes of the larvae. Although giant mealworms seem more easily digested by anurans than common mealworms, neither species should be fed in excess.

Mealworms

Long a favorite of neophyte reptile and amphibian keepers, mealworms (*Tenebrio molitor*) contain a great deal of chitin and should be fed sparingly. They are easily kept and bred in plastic receptacles containing a 2- to 3-inch (5–7.6 cm) layer of bran (available at livestock feed stores). A potato or an apple will satisfy their moisture requirements.

Roaches

Although roaches can be bred, it is nearly as easy to collect them as needed. Roaches, of one or more species, are present over much of the world. The size of the roach proffered must be tailored to the size of the amphibian being fed. A meal of several small roaches is usually better for your specimen than a meal of one or two large roaches.

Termites

Collect termites fresh as needed. Should you decide to hold "extras" over, they may be kept in some of the slightly dampened wood in which you originally found them. Termites are most easily collected during the damp weather of spring and early summer. One hobbyist has placed a huge pile of wood shavings some distance from his home and

Although an excellent food for small frogs, termites are extremely risky. They must not be allowed to escape in your home!

introduced termites to the pile. There the little insects can be collected nearly year round. (We must mention, however, that this approach to breeding termites has resulted in a permanent termite infestation in his house!) It is definitely best to collect these insects as needed, then use them immediately. Termites are among the best of foods for small frogs, toads, and treefrogs.

Fruit Flies

Breeding your own: Breeding stock of these tiny dipterids can be purchased from a biological supply house or collected from the wild. Biological supply houses will be able to supply you with flightless "vestigial-winged" fruit flies. The genetic mutation makes handling this insect much easier. Mashed fruit and agar (a seaweed derivative) are good foods. If you use flying species, have fly swatters handy.

Houseflies

These may be collected as needed (weather allowing) in commercial fly-traps or bred. Tightly covered, wide-mouthed gallon jars are ideal for the latter purpose (be sure to punch air

Even pests like houseflies can be fed to many frogs.

holes through the lid). The larvae (maggots) will thrive in putrefying meat, overripe fruit and vegetables, or other such media. Both larvae and adult flies can be fed to your specimens. The simplest method of introducing the adult flies to the cage is to place the opened jar inside the cage. This method allows fewer to escape. The maggots can be removed by hand or with forceps and placed in a shallow dish in the amphibian tank.

Mice

Many of the largest frogs and toads will relish adult mice, and even moderately sized amphibian specimens will accept nestling mice.

Mice of suitable sizes can be purchased at pet stores or bred at home.

Breeding your own: Mice are easily bred. A colony consisting of a single male and three or four females in a 10-gallon (38 L) tank (or a rodent-breeding cage) will produce a rather steady supply of babies that can be fed to your various amphibian species. (The mouse colony will produce a distinct odor, so locate the cages away from your home, in your garage, perhaps.) Giant toads, bullfrogs, and other large anurans will thrive on a diet of mice.

Use aspen or pine shavings for mouse bedding. Feed your mice either a "lab-chow" diet specifically formulated for them or a healthy mixture of seeds and vegetables. Fresh water must be present at all times.

Our tip: Do not use cedar bedding for your mice! The phenol contained in cedar is harmful to amphibians.

Health Hints and Medications

Frogs, toads, and treefrogs are creatures to be appreciated visually, *not handled.* Their delicate skin requires a degree of moisture and may be easily injured. Conversely, the toxins contained in the skin of some species can cause *you* harm. The message is: whenever possible just look, don't touch. If it becomes necessary to move a specimen, do so with extreme care. Small specimens can be shepherded into a fine-meshed net or a disposable plastic cup. Larger specimens can be grasped firmly, but gently, in the hand. Frogs and toads should be held at the waist. Aquatic specimens are best caught in an aquarium fish net of suitable size.

When it becomes necessary to handle them, amphibians must be grasped firmly but gently.

Our tip: No frogs are more difficult to restrain than the aquatic African clawed frogs, *Xenopus* sp. The skin exudates of these creatures are so slimy that restraining them in your hand may be next to impossible. These active, agile frogs can easily jump from a net. When transporting them *tightly and firmly* cover the net the frogs are in with a second net.

Proper Hygiene

Scrupulous cleanliness will do more to protect your frogs, toads, and treefrogs from illness than any other effort.

If kept clean and at temperatures suitable for the species involved, anurans are remarkably resistant to diseases and illnesses.

The single most prevalent cause of illness and disease in amphibians is poor husbandry. Lack of cleanliness or adverse cage temperature figure somewhere in about 95 percent of amphibian problems. All amphibians have a permeable skin that allows impurities from the container in which they are kept to enter the body rapidly and readily. It is impossible to overemphasize the necessity for cleanliness in an amphibian enclosure.

Ailments

"Redleg"

This bacterial disease can prove rapidly fatal. Because it is communicable, isolation of infected frogs is essential. The pathogen aeromonas is often, but not always implicated. Cleanliness and a suitable temperature regime will nearly always prevent this disease; conversely, fouled water or land areas and inordinate chill will assure its onset. Tetracycline hydrochloride is an often-used home remedy, but treatments performed by a qualified reptile veterinarian would be better. Cuts, scrapes, and lesions may be of mechanical or bacterial origin. For the first two types of injuries, a mild antibiotic salve may hasten healing, and the removal of the object that caused the injury will prevent recurrence. Veterinary assessment is suggested for lesions. The causative agent must be isolated and identified.

Aquatic frogs are best handled in nets.

Intestinal Impaction

If an overzealous frog ingests gravel or sand while feeding, intestinal impaction may occur. Small amounts of sand or an isolated small piece of gravel will usually be passed without any need for intervention. Larger impactions may require surgical removal.

Blindness

Quite recently a form of blindness caused by lipid buildups on the corneas has been seen in insectivorous frog species (*Litoria caerulea* among them) fed an excess of pink mice. No remedy has been found, but a suitable diet would seem to be the solution.

Fungus Infections

Fungi (usually a *Saprolegnia* sp.) may infect the wounds or scrapes of aquatic or principally aquatic frog species. The infection can be treated topically by removing the specimen from the water and daubing mercurochrome (2 percent), hydrogen peroxide (full strength), or malachite green (2 percent) on the area with a cotton pad.

Metabolic Bone Disease (MBD)

MBD may occur in amphibians that are provided insufficient calcium and vitamin D_3 additives in their diet. This is especially true in rapidly growing young animals. The method of prevention is simple—feed calcium and vitamin D_3 enhanced diets. The cure is less simple. Once sufficiently advanced to be observable, the insidious progression of this deficiency may not be reversible. Consult a veterinarian about injectable calcium treatments. It is possible that they will help.

Endoparasites

Frogs, toads, and treefrogs may host, among others, roundworms, tapeworms, pinworms, and flukes. Because of the virulence of the treatment and the small size of most amphibians, we strongly recommend consulting a veterinarian for both diagnosis and treatment.

Our tip: We suggest further that you find a qualified reptile/amphibian veterinarian before you actually need one. It may be too late to do so when your frog is ailing.

Breeding Suggestions

Reproductive Behavior

Although many of the species accounts (see pages 40 to 99) deal with the specifics of breeding particular anurans, some general rules apply to all of them.

Breeding is seasonal, and the trigger for breeding behavior is a combination of lessened or increased humidity and day-length changes. In the wild, of course, these conditions occur as the seasons change. In captivity, they must be duplicated.

The males of most anurans indicate their willingness to breed by their chorus. They sing both to warn other males and to attract females. Females, attracted by the males' songs, join them at the pond edge, the stream edge, or the ephemeral pool. If a female finds a particular male attractive—or if she's too slow to move away when approached—she will be clasped from behind by the male in a grip called "amplexus." Some males grasp by the waist, a practice that is called inguinal or pelvic amplexus; other male species grasp just behind the front legs, which is called axillary amplexus.

As her eggs are released, the male fertilizes them. For most toads, the eggs are in long strings; for most frogs and treefrogs, the eggs are in masses.

Development of the Eggs

The eggs of some species undergo direct development. Tiny froglets emerge from the egg capsule. The eggs of those species that go through a free-swimming tadpole stage remain submerged in the water or in above-water nests until the tadpoles hatch. Depending on the species, hatching may take as little as a day or considerably longer. At all times the water quality must be maintained. Filtration or daily partial water changes will help ensure this. The water temperature must be appropriate for the species. Normal room temperature is usually satisfactory for the incubation of the eggs of temperate or high-altitude species, while warmer temperatures must be provided for the eggs of tropical frogs.

As the hours pass, the eggs will change from a tiny circular blob in the center of a patch of clear gel to a less distinct tadpole-shaped blob in a clear gel. Unfertilized eggs will turn white and may "fuzz up" with fungus. You can remove these infertile eggs manually or leave them in place until the fertilized eggs hatch. Once the tadpoles wriggle free of the encasing gel, you'll need to begin feeding them, as they rapidly use up their reserve yolk. Raising tadpoles is achievable if food levels and water quality are maintained and space factors are considered.

The Tadpoles

When We Were Very Young . . .

Tadpoles—pollywogs—those tiny, tailed aquatic creatures that look like gigantic animated commas are well known to almost any boy or girl who has had an opportunity to explore a small country puddle or pond edge. Many of us, while growing up, had a favorite "frog pond" that we visited occasionally. We would trek a mile or

Cycling Your Frog, Toad, or Treefrog for Breeding

The breeding of many frogs, toads, and treefrogs may require a little more preparation than their everyday husbandry. This preparation, termed "cycling," relates directly to the conditions your specimens would experience in the natural world. The cycling procedure will vary according to the area to which your specimen is native. The following are guidelines only; you will have to tailor the overall procedure to fit the needs of your anurans.

For a period of 60 to 90 days during the winter months . . .

Specimens from	Wet tropics	Dry tropics	Wet temperate	Dry temperate	High elevations
will require cooling to:					
65–72°F (18.5–21.5°C)	X				
70–74°F (21–23.5°C)		X			
52–65°F (10.5–18.5°C)			X	X	X
Reduced relative humidity	X	X	X	X	X
Reduced actual humidity	X	X	X	X	X
Reduced feeding	X	X	X	X	X

Following the completion of the above, to stimulate reproductive readiness . . .

	Wet tropics	Dry tropics	Wet temperate	Dry temperate	High elevations
Warm to Normal room temperature	X	X	X	X	X
Increased relative humidity	X	X	X	X	X
Increased actual humidity	X	X	X	X	X
Increased feedings	X	X	X	X	X

Two weeks later . . .

	Wet tropics	Dry tropics	Wet temperate	Dry temperate	High elevations
Use hydration chamber	X	X	X	X	X

The shrill, chick-like peeps of the tiny, southeastern (USA) oak toad, Bufo quercicus, *are often heard during and following hard summer rains.*

The eggs of most toads are laid in strings. These are the eggs of the western toad, Bufo boreas, *in a mountain tarn.*

so along a silted, meandering woodland stream to a point where it puddled out onto a flattened expanse of land, pooling and deepening there before continuing to its exitway, where it dripped unevenly over trees placed across the streambed long ago. The chinks in those uneven trunks were filled with the fallen leaves of many autumns and at that point the water was about a foot and a half (about a half meter) deep. Tiny minnows swirled in the sunlight, flashing scales silver in the light, and an occasional newt would wriggle from the depths and ascend for a breath of air.

But better than those things were the tadpoles. Some years there were few; other years the muddy bottom of that pool fairly seethed with motion as these little beings went about the complex business of survival. Most had fat and rounded contours; a few had the nubbins of hindlegs, and toward autumn

Breeding discoglossid frogs indulge in inguinal (pelvic) amplexus, as shown by these oriental fire-bellied toads, Bombina orientalis.

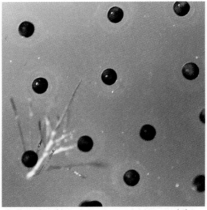

Cuban treefrog eggs are a common sight in flooded urban ditches.

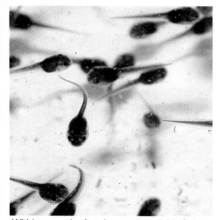

Within a week after the eggs are laid, Cuban treefrog hatchlings have assumed the typical tadpole shape—that of a swimming comma.

This green frog tadpole, Rana clamitans melanota, *has developed both fore and rear limbs.*

there was an occasional tadpole with one or both forelegs in evidence.

Most of us didn't know then what kind of tadpoles those were. To the kids that frequented the environs of that little frog pond the tadpoles were those of "bullfrogs." But then, except for the "hoptoads," all other frogs that we saw in those long-ago days were bullfrogs.

At some time during almost every year most of us would grab a can from a nearby dump, gather up a few of those tadpoles and trudge homeward with a cherished cargo. Once home we would dig out the "big" goldfish bowl, toss in a bottom covering of pebbles and a sprig or two of cabomba (if we had had the foresight to gather it with the tadpoles), add water, tadpoles, then sit back and watch, and watch, and watch. We would change the water occasionally ("when it got dirty" was the criterion applied), but despite this very unscientific approach, the tadpoles lived—thrived for that matter.

We knew from watching the tadpoles in their pond that they actively foraged in and on algal mats, dead tadpoles, and frogs and mucked about in the bottom mulm. Feeding them was pretty straightforward. Algae was never hard to get. We just hiked back to the pond and gathered it when necessary. Our tadpoles would also eagerly consume an occasional dead worm, an even more occasional piece of meat, and goldfish food. The diet seemed fine. The tadpoles lived and grew.

The nubbin of a tail still showing on this metamorphosing green frog, Rana clamitans melanota, *will soon be entirely resorbed. The tail is the only remnant of its tadpole life.*

Those of us who enjoyed watching the sequence of events always tried to get the smaller tadpoles, those without even the vestiges of hind legs. That way we had nearly a full summer of tadpole watching ahead of us. We could watch the buds of the hind legs appear and develop. Later, first one forelimb would appear, then the other. The little terminal mouth with its black scraping excrescences would widen . . . widen . . . widen, finally to be replaced by the ear-to-ear grinning maw of a frog. At that stage the tadpole would zoom ever more frequently to the surface to grab a hurried breath, the tail would get smaller and smaller, and the little creature would give up its place on the bottom to nestle close to the floating water plants in its bowl. The small, laterally situated eyes would develop eyelids and almost overnight (it seemed) become the protuberant pop eyes of the adult. Finally the hind limbs would become more muscular, the tail would be entirely resorbed, and, *voilá*, a baby frog! Nature was, indeed, wonderful!

Identifying Tadpoles

Although today Patti and I are well aware of the diversity of frogdom (meaning that not all are "bullfrogs" any more), we still thoroughly enjoy watching the developmental stages of a tadpole; and despite our somewhat greater level of sophistication, most are still "pollywogs"! But now they're green frog (or *Rana clamitans*) pollywogs (like those of our childhood were), or gray treefrog (*Hyla versicolor*) pollywogs, or southern toad (*Bufo terrestris*) pollywogs.

Most current field guides contain a key to help you identify at least a few of these difficult little creatures. Such a key was one of the noteworthy additions to the latest edition of the Peterson Field Guide series entitled *Reptiles and Amphibians, Eastern/ Central North America*, by Roger Conant and Joseph T. Collins. Tadpole identification is also carried in the Western field guide of the same series, by Robert C. Stebbins (see page 100).

Tadpoles remain tough to identify, but at least we now know how to do so if necessary.

As you might have surmised, tadpoles are not difficult to hatch and rear. Most common forms will succumb to, or be deformed by, acidic water conditions. In some areas that are very prone to acidification of water, this man-made phenomenon, either singly or in combination with other, less-understood, atmospheric alterations, has caused the virtual disappearance of once-common species of frogs, toads, and treefrogs. Other, always-less-common, species are on the verge of extinction.

Because of this and a heightened awareness of the benefits afforded our planet by the tailless amphibians, many kinds of frogs, toads, and treefrogs are now granted protection at state or federal levels or both. Check applicable state laws before collecting any specimens.

Although most tadpoles are compatible if fed well, those of many species will become cannibalistic if perpetually hungry or crowded. The tadpoles of some species are more prone to cannibalism than those of others. (Mention of the most likely offenders will be made in appropriate species accounts.)

Since filtration does much to overcome many smaller mistakes and oversights, we feel it is an important addition to the tadpole aquarium. For the basics in setting up your aquarium, refer to page 18. One word of caution: For several days after hatching, tadpoles are weak swimmers. Tailor any pumps and filters accordingly. If the current and intake are too strong, your tadpoles may be carried into or against the filter or intake and be injured or killed.

Today an ever-increasing number of herpetoculturists are breeding tailless amphibians. Although the tadpoles of many species are kept communally, those of others seem to do best if isolated—one or two per container. When small numbers of a small species (arrow-poison frogs, mantellas, etc.) are involved, the tadpoles can be maintained from hatching to metamorphosis in styrofoam or plastic drinking cups. Manual cleaning is necessary at two-day intervals. When larger numbers of tadpoles are involved it may become necessary, or at least desirable, to design an automated system. Such systems can be simple or complex. Automated systems involve devising a setup that will allow the water to flow through many cups simultaneously. A recirculation system seems ideal and an in-line filtration system is essential. A plastic blanket box or some other easily cleaned, durable container can be used as the main reservoir (in which the tadpole-holding cups are set). In and out water lines can be cemented in place. The water will need to be changed every two or three days, at which time the entire system should be scrubbed, sterilized, and refilled.

The communal rearing of large numbers of tadpoles, whatever the species, is the easiest method but *will* require a large volume of water. A children's wading pool, although not decorative, can accommodate such a volume, is inexpensive, and is very easy to work with. Depending on the size of the pool as well as the size and the number of tadpoles involved, one partial and one complete water change a week may be necessary for the entire developmental timespan. The quality of your water will dictate the frequency and degree of changes. A good filtration system will help decrease the amount of care necessary.

Beside algae, many tadpoles will eat such animal matter as blood, black and white worms, finely chopped earthworms, and—in a pinch—very finely chopped raw beef heart. Uneaten food should be removed within a few hours. If it is left to putrefy, the water quality will quickly be affected.

The tadpoles of some species (such as clawed frogs, *Xenopus* sp.) are plankton feeders. Suggestions for caring for these specialized species appear within the text account for each species.

With ample water quantity, good water quality, and proper feeding, tadpoles of many frogs, toads, and treefrogs can be metamorphosed in four to six weeks after hatching. Some may take longer, especially at cool temperatures; some, like the tadpoles of the Malayan painted frog, may metamorphose in only two weeks.

The raising of tadpoles can be a "watch, learn, and enjoy" project for children and adults alike.

The Flat-tongued Frogs: Family Discoglossidae

The Fire-bellied Toads

If brilliantly hued amphibians appeal to you, you'll probably enjoy keeping the fire-bellied toads of the genus *Bombina*. All member species are small, very attractive, responsive, easily maintained, and long-lived. All may be kept with other *Bombina*. Be aware, however, that like many other small frogs and toads, they will hybridize; you may wish to separate them during breeding season.

Species Accounts

Although there are some half dozen species of fire-bellied toads, only three are seen in herpetoculture with any degree of regularity. One of them, the Oriental fire-bellied toad, *Bombina orientalis*, is a mainstay of the pet industry. The other two, which are occasionally encountered, are the common or European fire-bellied toad, *B. bombina*, and the yellow-bellied toad, *B. variegatus*, also of Europe. (Rarely, a small shipment of a fourth species, the interesting and very glandular *B. maxima*, may be available in the pet market.)

Appearance: Actually, besides being the most common, the Oriental fire-bellied toad is also the most attractively colored of the trio. As a matter of fact, few anuran species can outdo the brilliant hues of the Oriental fire-belly. With its dorsum of black-mottled lime green (the lime coloration can dull to olive on occasion) and venter of black reticulated red-orange, this little discoglossid (meaning "flat-tongued") is a pretty sight whether viewed from above or below. Those we maintain spend hours sitting on their driftwood rafts or atop the mat of *Hydrilla* that floats in their tank.

The half dozen Oriental fire-bellies share their 20-gallon (75 L) long tank with three European fire-bellied and three yellow-bellied toads, species that are gray to olive gray dorsally. The European fire-bellies have dark dorsal markings, most often in the form of rather regularly spaced, elongate ovals. The dark markings are nearly lacking on the unrelieved gray to olive gray dorsa of the yellow-bellied toads.

The bellies of the two species are different as well. The venters of the European fire-bellied toads are predominantly dark with flame red

The black markings on the dorsa of Oriental fire-bellied toads, Bombina orientalis, *are variable both in size and number.*

The common European fire-bellied toad, Bombina bombina, *takes its common name from its brilliantly colored venter.*

blotches; those of the yellow-bellied toads are predominantly yellow with dark reticulations. When viewed from above, the snout of the yellow-bellied toad is seen to be considerably more bluntly rounded than the snout of the European fire-bellied species.

Color and toxicity: As is usually the case, the brilliant aposematic coloration of the fire-bellied toads is indicative of either actual toxicity or acrid taste. When any of our *Bombina* accidentally would mouth the foot or leg of another during the excitement of being offered earthworms, the grasp was quickly released. If ever a look of anticipation could be replaced by disgust in an amphibian's face, it was then. After the release, the toad that had done the grasping would close its eyes, lower its head, wipe its mouth with its forefeet and move rapidly away from the animal it had grasped.

If surprised away from water or grasped by a larger predator, all bombina indulge in the *unken* (boat) reflex. In this, the back is bowed and the legs raised upward, fully revealing the brilliant flash colors. Occasionally the frogs may actually turn upside down in their efforts to display their warning. Most predators that do not understand the message will quickly drop the bite-sized toads once the whitish, latexlike skin secretions are exuded.

Frightened fire-bellied toads often curve their body and legs upwards in an effort to display the brilliant colors that denote toxicity. This yellow-bellied toad, Bombina variegatus, *is assuming the posture.*

41

Diet: All three of these *Bombina* species are avid feeders, especially fond of small earthworms or sections of larger earthworms. These toads also consume vitamin-dusted crickets of suitable size as well as waxworms and butterworms. The sections of larger earthworms are proffered in "bite-sized" sections impaled on broomstraws. Although labor-intensive, this method of feeding serves two purposes. It allows "quantity control," enabling you to ensure that each toad gets ample food, and it also allows your animals to become accustomed to your presence. Within a matter of days, fire-bellied toads that were entirely wild when received would crowd around the front of their tank when we approached.

Caging: Fire-bellied toads adapt well to life in either a semiaquatic terrarium or a well-planted aquarium with floating vegetation and a haulout raft. A suitably sized piece of corkbark will suffice for the raft.

Many frogs will accept pieces of worms that have been impaled on a broomstraw. Be careful that the end of the straw does not protrude below the segment.

If you use the aquarium setup, you must pay as much attention to water quality as you would if keeping fish. Chlorine and chloramine, ammonia, and other "purifiers" and by-products must be removed. In our aquariums we maintain the water level about 3 inches (7.6 cm) below the top of the tank, a level entirely achievable with outside filters. There is plenty of headroom for the toads after they have emerged from the water.

Both terrarium and aquarium should be provided with dual fluorescent tube lighting, one a plant "grow" tube and the other a full spectrum tube. Room temperature of 68 to 80°F (16–27°C) is fine for these toads.

Although the various fire-bellied toads are less adept at climbing terrarium glass than many other amphibians, if conditions are right (humidity, etc.), they still may occasionally ascend to the top of the tank, especially in the corners. Thus, a terrarium top is essential.

Breeding: The various fire-bellied toads can be bred in captivity. Cycling *B. bombina* and *B. variegata* (species from more temperate climes) for breeding is somewhat different from the procedure used for the Chinese *B. orientalis*. For the two former species, a darkened hibernation period of between 60 and 90 days at 40 to 45°F (4–7°C) apparently is necessary to induce ovulation and spermatogenesis the following spring. The Oriental fire-bellied toad requires a similar period of cooling, but winter temperatures in the mid-60s F to very low 70s F (18–22°C) seem to suffice.

Both breeding and release calls of the males of the several species of fire-bellied toads are variations of the same theme, a low-pitched, soft, but not unmusical "whoop, whoop, whoop." The release call is voiced when an amorous male grasps another male. The call, in combination with body vibrations, indicates to the grasping male his mistake. The vibrations are also produced by nonreceptive females when they are grasped. The breeding grasp (amplexus) is inguinal (pelvic).

The 50 to 225 eggs of fire-bellied toads are usually attached to submerged anchors. Plant stems, twigs, limbs, grasses, and rocks are commonly used. The eggs may be single, in small clusters, or in sizable clumps.

Tadpoles: The tiny (¼ inch or .6 cm) larvae hatch some three to six days following egg deposition. Like most anuran hatchlings, the tadpoles of fire-bellied toads are inactive at first. They will adhere in a vertical position to the aquarium glass or submerged plants, rocks, or twigs for several days. After utilizing their contained yolk, the tadpoles will begin searching for tiny particles of food. The very finest of prepared, powdered fish-fry food, strained pond plankton, and chopped tubifex and bloodworms are acceptable.

If fed heavily the tadpoles will grow and develop quickly, metamorphosing in about a month. After the forelimbs appear, it will be necessary to provide heavy mats of floating plants or small islands of cork or styrofoam for the toadlets to clamber upon. We prefer the matted floating plants, which may also be utilized by the tadpoles.

Toadlets: Dully colored at metamorphosis, many toadlets born in captivity never develop a bright belly. The youngsters may not feed for a day or two following their emergence from the water. However, when they do start to eat, they will require vast quantities of "pinhead" sized crickets, fruit flies, springtails, and other tiny insect prey. They would probably enjoy earthworms as well, but we couldn't figure out how to impale a piece of earthworm small enough for their very tiny mouths.

It is important that the newly emerged toads not be crowded. Ten or a dozen babies to a 10-gallon (38 L) aquarium seem to fare far better than when all are kept together in a larger tank.

Aquarium Favorites: Family Pipidae

The Tongueless Frogs

Often one's introduction to the hobby of keeping frogs, toads, and treefrogs occurs while browsing at an aquarium shop. Among the tanks of fish specialties, it is not uncommon to encounter tanks containing a half dozen or more fingernail-sized frogs that scoot in little bursts of speed around the bottom in search of food or dart upward for a breath of air. Many people, enchanted by the actions of these little underwater beings, return home with a couple, not knowing much about them—other than that they are small and interesting and were kept by the pet store with several kinds of fish.

If the aquarist was lucky, the animals he or she acquired were dwarf underwater frogs. These stay small and tractable and continue to entertain without problem. However, if the hobbyist was unlucky, the animals were clawed frogs. Clawed frogs would settle in and begin to grow, and grow, and grow, while the tropical fish in the tank would begin to disappear. Sooner or later the frogs would become suspect, and eventually the suspicion would be confirmed when a frog was discovered with the tail of one of its finned tankmates still protruding from its mouth.

At that point, one of two things usually happened. With a belated cry of anguish, the aquarist removed the frogs, which were returned with dispatch to the shop from which they came (and which now hesitated to accept them), or a frog tank was set up and the start of a new hobby and new interest ensued.

The two frog species frequently seen in aquarium stores both belong to the family Pipidae (the tongueless frogs) but represent two different genera. The smaller of the two is appropriately known as the dwarf underwater frog, *Hymenochirus curtipes*. The larger form is the clawed frog, *Xenopus laevis*, so called for the horny toe caps it bears. (There are other species in both genera, but they are seldom available in the pet trade.) When they are small, their care is identical.

These interesting animals both originate in Africa. The dwarf species

The dwarf underwater frog, Hymenochirus curtipes, *has webbed front feet.*

is more tropical, requiring the warmth typical of tropical fish tanks. The clawed frog, from a region much farther south, is capable of withstanding temperatures somewhat higher, and very much lower, for varying durations. Notwithstanding its tolerance of such extremes, the clawed frog also does best at tropical tank temperatures.

Dwarf Underwater Frogs

These popular aquarium frogs are adult at between ¾ and 1¼ inches (about 2–3.1 cm) in length. Tiny, dark, clawlike toe-tip excrescences are present on the three inner toes of each rear foot.

Appearance: Despite having a flattened countenance, dwarf underwater frogs are of rather normal appearance. The eyes are situated and directed laterally, the hind limbs are powerfully developed, and the forefeet are webbed. Their skin is somewhat roughened (granular), making them easily held. They are olive-green to olive-brown, usually with a profusion of dark speckling dorsally. The sides may show a vague peach coloration. Albinos have been seen, but for some reason the aberrancy has not yet been established.

Sexing: The female is the larger sex. Males may be easily determined by the presence of a small elongate sacklike gland (the postaxillary gland) immediately behind each forelimb. The function of these glands is unknown, but since they are in contact with the female during breeding, they are thought to provide a stimulatory effect upon her. The males vocalize with a quick series of clicks, which can be heard beyond their tanks.

Diet: *Hymenochirus*, at all stages of their lives, will eagerly consume bloodworms, whiteworms, tubifex worms, and finely chopped earthworms. Some prepared fish foods and softened

Albino African clawed frogs, Xenopus laevis, *have long been bred for both the pet trade and medical purposes.*

Reptomin sticks are also accepted. As tadpoles, they are carnivorous and will consume tiny microorganisms such as infusoria, graduating to copepods, daphnia, and tiny aquatic worms as size permits.

Clawed Frogs

The clawed frog is now established in certain areas of southern California and has been found (but is not yet

The normal African clawed frog is also readily available to hobbyists and medical researchers.

known to be established) in southern Florida. A single specimen (obviously an escapee) was seen in Colorado swimming in a pool so cold that it had begun to ice over. Under such frigid conditions the dwarf underwater frog would have been long dead; the clawed frog is vastly more temperature-tolerant.

Appearance: The dorsally directed, lidless eyes of the clawed frogs seem to scan the heavens. Dorsolateral ridges run the length of their body in a series of glandular "puckers" reminiscent of seams sewn by a novice tailor. The front toes are not webbed, though the rear ones are. The inner three rear toes are tipped with horny claws.

Sexing: The females are the larger sex, occasionally nearing 5 inches (12.7 cm) in SVL. Sexually mature females have easily seen cloacal papillae. Reproductively active males develop dark, roughened, nuptial pad-like excrescences on the fingers and forearms that help them retain their grip while amplexing. The males produce a series of rapid clicks that are easily heard beyond the confines of their tanks.

Diet: Because of their much larger size, adult clawed frogs will eagerly consume a mix of small goldfish, earthworms, Reptomin, beef heart, and other such fare.

Considerations for Both *Hymenochirus curtipes* and *Xenopus laevis*

Caging: Neither the underwater nor the clawed frogs require landing or "haulout" areas for any part of their life cycle. We furnish a rather thick pebble substrate. We also provide the dwarf underwater frogs with a profusion of aquatic plants, either floating or rooted, and the tiny frogs both rest in and forage actively among their leaves and stems. Because of the efficiency and persistence with which the larger *Xenopus* go about rearranging the landscaping contours of their aquarium, we supply them only with floating plants. Even those soon show signs of wear and need replacing.

Of course, neither species requires plants; we simply prefer them for aesthetic reasons. Besides plants, we use leached driftwood and unmovable rocks (placed flat on the bottom glass) for tank decoration.

Breeding: Both species are hardy, easily kept, and fairly long lived; both are readily bred in captivity. Reproductive readiness can be stimulated either naturally or hormonally. Usually the natural method is used with the dwarf underwater frog, the hormonal with the clawed frog.

Natural stimulation is simply accomplished. In their natural habitats the reproductive sequences of both *Hymenochirus* and *Xenopus* are stimulated by the freshening of their ponds and puddles by rain. The rapid drop in water temperature associated with heavy rain is probably as important as the freshening itself. Reproduction of these frogs in captivity may be stimulated by replacing half or more of the aquarium water with water 12 to 15°F (5–8°C) cooler. The rapid change will almost always stimulate the dwarf frogs to breed and will often succeed with the clawed frogs as well.

The methods of reproduction are interesting and rather complex. Amplexus is inguinal (pelvic); the male grasps the female around her waist. The nuptial excrescences aid the male greatly in retaining his hold. (This is especially useful with *Xenopus*, a frog with such slippery skin that it is almost impossible to hold it in your hand!). While amplexing, the pair moves in an arc upward to the top of the water. Once there, while in an inverted (venter up) position, the first batch of eggs is laid and fertilized. The eggs float at the surface. Following oviposition the two frogs complete their aquatic arc, returning to the bottom of the tank. The sequence will be repeated several to many times and many hundreds of eggs will ultimately be laid.

The blocky, rather sedentary tadpoles of the dwarf underwater frogs are as different in appearance from the sleek active ones of the clawed frog as the two adults are from one another. Both tadpole species are carnivorous, mid-water feeders, avidly consuming zooplankton. (See pages 38 and 39 for suggestions on raising tadpoles.)

Caution: The keeping of clawed frogs (*Xenopus*) may be illegal in some states. Be certain to check existing fish and game laws before purchasing any.

Surinam Toads

On the opposite side of the globe from the clawed and dwarf frogs there exists one of the strangest of the world's anurans: the Surinam toad, *Pipa pipa.*

Appearance: The Surinam toad is unique among anurans. One's initial response to seeing a Surinam is to think that the creature somehow survived a devastating encounter with a car. The entire animal is dorsoventrally flattened, and from each of the four corners of its rather squared body protrudes a leg. The rear legs are heavily muscled and the feet are fully webbed. The toad is a powerful swimmer. The forelimbs, small and weak in appearance, extend anterior to the head whether the toad is resting or swimming. The front feet have no webs; the fingers are clustered and directed anteriorly, and each finger terminates in a tiny star of integument that is highly enervated, hence sensory. The eyes of the Surinam toad are tiny, lidless, and directed upward, giving the toad a "star-gazing" appear-

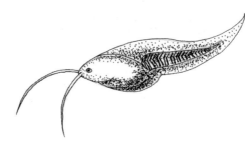

Paired tentacles identify the active tadpoles of the clawed frog.

ance. Although the toad is tongueless, food items—aquatic insects, worms, tadpoles, small fish, and other tiny aquatic creatures—are swept into the wide mouth by the forelimbs.

Diet: Surinam toads are easily maintained in the home. As long as there is no great disparity in size, Surinams may be maintained as individuals, in groups, or with clawed frogs in suitably sized aquariums. Food items for the toads include earthworms, grubs, tadpoles, and small fish. (It has been suggested that certain elements present in goldfish may be detrimental to the health of some of the predatory species to which goldfish are routinely fed. To preclude the possibility of harm, we generally offer Surinam toads only "feeder" tropical fish and suitably sized bait fish.)

Caging: Although the dwarf underwater frogs would be immediately consumed if kept with the larger frog species, a very attractive setup that accommodates dwarf and clawed frogs and Surinam toads can easily be arranged by dividing a large tank. With today's silicone sealants, this is an easy task. Merely cut a piece of glass that is both as tall and as long (in terms of inside dimensions) as your tank. Cement this in place about one third of the distance from back to front. The seal *must* be complete on both ends and the bottom. When it has cured, fill, plant, and filter the back partition as you would any other aquarium. This will be the home of your dwarf frogs. The two larger species will live in the larger front section. Separate filtration will be necessary.

With a little work and imagination, a truly innovative setup—your own little combination of Amazonia and Africa—can be created, easily maintained, and thoroughly enjoyed.

Breeding: There are, in fact, at least three species in the genus *Pipa.* Of these it is *Pipa pipa* that is available in the pet industry. Thus, when the somewhat generic term "Surinam toad" is mentioned, it is usually *Pipa pipa* that is meant. All three *Pipa* are remarkable not only for their appearance, but for their breeding biology as well. No account of the Surinam toad(s), however cursory, would be complete without a mention of the latter.

During a rather complex breeding sequence, the fertilized eggs are placed on the back of the female toad. The dorsal skin becomes highly vascularized and soon grows around and over the ova, which, in time, hatch. In some species of *Pipa*, the young emerge as tadpoles. In *Pipa pipa*, the young fully metamorphose while in their protective pocket. The juveniles, tiny replicas of the 6-inch (15.2 cm) long adults, emerge, disperse, and begin lives of their own.

The flattened, entirely aquatic, neotropical Surinam toad, Pipa pipa, *is one of the strangest of all anurans in appearance.*

The eastern spadefoot, Scaphiopus h. holbrooki, *is one of the most secretive of anurans. Vertically elliptical pupils indicate its strongly nocturnal tendencies.*

The Malayan horned frog, Megophrys nasuta, *is a voracious predator of large insects and smaller frogs. In captivity it requires cool and very clean caging.*

Burrowers: Family Pelobatidae

The Spadefoots

Although spadefoots, or spadefoot toads, are common to abundant over much of their range, so secretive are these nocturnal burrowing anurans that their presence is often unsuspected. In one or another of their several species, spadefoots may be encountered from extreme south central Canada to central Mexico. The eastern spadefoot is the only member found east of the Mississippi, from central New England to the Florida Keys.

Spadefoots are pelobatid ("digging") toads of well-drained sandy habitats. All are usually considered members of the genus *Scaphiopus* (although some researchers believe that differences among the species warrant a second genus, *Spea*).

Finding a Spadefoot

Frequently, the first indication that spadefoots exist in a neighborhood is the sighting of one in a cellar window well, hatchway, or cellar itself. Spadefoots often tumble into such areas during their occasional nocturnal perambulations. There's another way of learning of the existence of spadefoots: Following or during torrential rains, the little (2 to 2.5 inch or 5–6.3 cm) toads emerge en masse from their subsurface hiding places to congregate and breed in puddles. Their vocalizations, often like a resounding chorus of hearty burps (no spadefoot has a musical call), can be nearly overwhelming.

Because they are so secretive, spadefoots are only occasionally offered by reptile dealers. Spadefoots are never expensive, but because they spend most of their time in sub-surface hiding places, few hobbyists are drawn to them. We find them interesting little creatures, but their general natural history and amazing ability to survive drought are better studied in the field than in captivity.

Appearance: Spadefoots can be easily mistaken for common toads. However, spadefoots have a less warty body, lack parotoid (shoulder) glands, and possess only a single horny spade (true toads have two) on each heel. Spadefoots also have vertically elliptical pupils, while those of true toads are horizontal.

The Eastern spadefoot, *S. h. holbrooki,* usually has a ground color of olive brown to deep brown and a lighter dorsal design in the form of an hourglass or lyre. Despite living in a region of high rainfall, this little toad inhabits only open field and meadows having extensive areas of sandy, well-drained soil. Where common, they may be plowed to the surface during agricultural preparations. They spend the winters deep in the ground, buried below the frost line.

Caging: Spadefoots need a terrarium with a deep covering of loose sandy soil on the bottom. The bottom layers of the substrate should be damp but the top layers rather dry. This can be easily accomplished, if your soil is deep enough, by inserting a hollow tube (pipe) through the soil to the bottom of the terrarium. Pouring water slowly into the tube will allow the moisture to dampen the lower layers and travel upward by capillary action. Thus the soil will be dampest on the bottom and driest on the top.

Breeding: Both the western and the eastern spadefoots breed in temporary puddles and ponds. The time between egg deposition and metamorphosis is more rapid than with most similarly sized frogs or toads that breed in permanent (or at least less ephemeral) locations. Cannibalism is well documented in the tadpoles of several spadefoot species.

The Malayan Horned Frog

A very interesting spadefoot relative occasionally offered for sale is the Malayan horned frog, *Megophrys nasuta*. (Do not confuse this old-world frog with the new-world tropical horned frogs of the genus *Ceratophrys*, discussed on page 52.) It is a persistently nocturnal frog of cool, damp Malaysian forests. Some authorities consider it a subspecies of the more widely ranging *M. monticola.*

Appearance: The Malayan horned frog is a pretty, but modestly colored species. It is typically clad dorsally in grays, tans, russets, or browns and is darker laterally. It has a large, angular head, adorned with a supraciliary projection above each eye and a prominent nasal projection as well. Sizable tubercles are present at the corners of the wide mouth. The various projections and cryptic coloration afford a resting horned frog an amazing degree of camouflage. Unless it is moving, this creature of the shadowy forest floor is easily overlooked. This frog that frequently eats other frog species, although it seems to be far less aggressive toward human fingers than other frogs are. Females occasionally attain more than 5 inches (12.7 cm) in snout-to-vent length. Males are seldom more than half that size.

Diet: Like many other big-headed frogs, the Malayan horned frog is highly predacious and quite voracious. It consumes, besides the typical arachnid and anellid fare, nestling rodents, lizards, and other frogs.

Caging: If kept in a cool, damp, well-planted (or otherwise shaded) semiaquatic terrarium, the Malayan horned frog is a hardy captive. It will utilize both land and water areas extensively. Overall cleanliness is very important if you intend to succeed with this species.

Breeding: This is the only pelobatid frog bred in captivity with any regularity. The female attaches her egg clusters to the underside of water-swept rocks and logs, which may be partially or entirely submerged. If the deposition site is submerged, the eggs hatch and the tadpoles are immediately at home. Should the waters have receded, leaving the deposition site above the surface, the tadpoles reportedly slide down to the water on threads of the thin, gelatinous egg covering. The eggs are large and relatively few in number.

The Wonderful Hopping Mouths: Family Leptodactylidae

The Horned Frogs

The horned frogs constitute a sub-family, the Ceratophryinae, within the family Leptodactylidae. The ceratophrines are all highly predacious Latin American species. Because the criteria used to designate species are in flux, the exact number of species in this intriguing genus is uncertain. Some favor placing the horned frogs and several closely related genera in a family of their own, the Ceratophryidae.

In 1985 the ornate horned frog was only beginning to become a popular pet, and the Chaco horned frog was

Big headed and short tempered, the ornate horned frog, Ceratophrys ornata, *may well be the most popular frog in the hobby. It is often called the "Pac Man frog."*

barely known. Today (1996) these two species, sold by pet shops as "Pac-Man" frogs, are the all-time favorites of hobbyists. Not only are both species readily available, but they have been interbred to produce albino Chaco horned frogs.

Certainly ease of care has contributed significantly to their popularity. But two other factors have also conspired: our fascination with the bizarre in appearance and our attraction to the notion of predator overcoming prey!

Frog folklore: In their native South America, horned frogs (*escuerzos*) are surrounded by myth. To them is attributed all of the lore that surrounds snapping turtles in the United States. Tales relating the ferocity of these frogs are widely spread, enhanced further in each telling. One tale claims that the frogs grab the lips of livestock grazing too close to them, then hang on until the hapless cow or horse dies of starvation; others tell of frogs that bite fingers and refuse to relinquish their grasp until sundown or, worse yet, of persons having to sever fingers to get a frog off, of venoms so potent that a bite means nearly instantaneous death—the tales go on and on.

The truth is that these frogs have perfected techniques of bluff and aggression to dissuade potential predators. Horned frogs huff, puff, open their capacious mouths in threat,

Once imported in large numbers, the small Colombian horned frog, Ceratophrys calcarata *is no longer a species frequently seen in herpetoculture.*

Albino Chacoan horned frogs, Ceratophrys cranwelli, *are now nearly as commonly seen in herpetoculture as normal colored examples.*

and jump forward and bite. The bite of these predatory frogs with greatly developed jaws is both disconcerting and uncomfortable. To add to the unpleasantness, they (and many other predacious frog species) have sharp jawbones studded with a number of small "teeth" as well as larger, cusp-like projections on their lower jaw. The projections (called odontoid structures) prevent prey animals (often other frogs, sometimes their keepers) from

escaping once grasped. As one might expect from their appearance, speed and agility are lacking in this corpulent species. Once you've worked with horned frogs, you'll agree they don't possess either of those attributes.

One day Patti was working in a fairly large pen in which we maintained several ornate horned frogs. Thinking all of the creatures had been transferred to an alternate pen, she brushed some overhanging grasses

A Chacoan horned frog with normal coloration.

The Surinam horned frog, Ceratophrys cornuta, *has the longest "horns" of the frogs in this genus.*

The comparative horn sizes of three horned frogs are seen here. Top to bottom, C. cranwelli, C. ornata, C. cornuta.

imprinted. I've had adult females (almost twice the size of the males) grab my fingers and have never failed to wonder why I was dumb enough to let that happen! It hurt!

So—horned frogs can and will bite. Large specimens of the larger species can easily kill and consume large mice or small rats!

Appearance: Horned frogs, genus *Ceratophrys*, derive their common name from the fleshy projection, a "horn," if you will, present on each upper eyelid. The projections vary in size from the barely discernible nubbins of the ornate horned frog, *C. ornata*, to the prominent projections on the eyelids of the Surinam horned frog, *C. aurita*. All horned frogs have sparsely to heavily tubercled skin. All have very large mouths.

Most hobbyists acquire their horned frogs as newly metamorphosed or small froglets. At that stage they are about 1 inch (2.5 cm) in length, big-headed, but rather slender-bodied. Little suggests the size they will attain. But one thing is common to both juveniles and adults: a grumpy disposition.

Species Accounts

The Brazilian horned frog: The largest species, the dinner-plate-sized *C. aurita*, is seldom seen, even in zoological gardens. However, other forms once rare in herpetoculture are now seen with regularity.

The ornate horned frog: Known also as the Argentine horned frog, *C. ornata* is usually well patterned with green, terra cotta, or a combination of both colors, against a lighter ground. The amount of pattern can vary considerably. Some specimens may be predominantly of the blotch color, others of the lighter ground color. Yellows, blacks, and browns can also be incorporated into the color scheme. Adult females are among the largest members of this genus. They may

out of the way—and with a holler yanked her hand quickly back. Not quickly enough, it turned out, for a large adult male horned frog had become firmly affixed to her fingers. When it realized its mistake, the frog quickly released its grip (no, Patti didn't have to await sundown), but a painful lesson had been indelibly exceed salad-plate size. Normally, they are even broader than they are long. Males are significantly smaller, often less than half the size of the females. Mature males have a suffusion of dark pigment on the throat.

The Chaco, or Cranwell's, horned frog: *C. cranwelli* is the second-most frequently seen species. Like the ornate, it is produced in large numbers in captive-breeding programs. Although many wild-caught specimens are of rather dull coloration, color enhancement through selective breeding has now produced some very pretty animals. Recently (1993) albino specimens became available. Already (1996) their prices have dropped, and albinos are hardly more expensive than specimens of normal color.

The Chaco horned frog is so similar to many ornate horned frogs in appearance that it was until recently thought to be merely a slightly divergent, big-headed morph of the ornate. The supraocular horn is also somewhat larger proportionally.

Surinam horned frog: Although at present it is only sporadically available, the prettily colored little Surinam horned frog, *C. cornuta,* occasionally appears on the pet market. Unfortunately, this is a species that prefers other frogs as prey. Only rarely will an imported wild adult voluntarily accept insects or mice as prey items. In fact, many Surinam horned frogs will steadfastly refuse food. Some never feed voluntarily; others may begin to eat after an initial period of force-feeding. To add to this problem, many of the imported Surinam horned frogs are severely infested with internal parasites (a common malady in frog-eating herps of many kinds), a problem that may be difficult to address. Obviously, freshly imported Surinam horned frogs usually are not easily kept by hobbyists. Fortunately, though, a few specimens have now been captive-bred and the babies seem somewhat more amenable to captive conditions than the imported adults.

Most female Surinam horned frogs are adult at less than a 3-inch (7.6 cm) body length. The males are smaller. This species is predominantly tan or buff and has a broad vertebral stripe of similar color. The sides and legs are patterned with blotches and stripes of darker colors. Occasional specimens have some lime green incorporated into the color scheme; these frogs, usually males, are very attractive. Males also have a suffusion of dusky pigment on the skin of their throats. The horns of this species are very well developed, in fact, more so than those of any other member of the genus.

Colombian horned frog: In bygone years a fourth species of horned frog was also abundantly available. This was the 3-inch (7.6 cm) long (males smaller) Colombian species, *C. calcarata.* Currently only a few captive-raised babies appear on the pet market annually. In this species too, the males tend to be more brightly colored than the females. Males also have a dark throat. Although not all imported specimens eat readily, most individuals of this species do eventually feed. Although they probably feed mostly on frogs in the wild, Colombian horned frogs are not so reluctant as the Surinam species to adjust to normally preferred food items. The supraocular projections of this species are only moderately developed.

Hybrids between the ornate and the Surinam, the Chaco and the Surinam, and the ornate and the Chaco horned frogs have been produced and are occasionally available. They are generally rather expensive, and we find them much less attractive than the true species. However, most hybrid horned frogs, even those involving the often problematic Surinam, feed well and are hardy.

Budgett's Frog

In recent months several representatives of the leptodactylid genus *Lepidobatrachus* have become rather readily available. Of these, two are true species and one is a naturally occurring hybrid that had for years been afforded its own specific name.

Lepidobatrachus laevis, commonly called the Budgett's frog, is another species with a perpetually aggressive attitude. At 4.5 inches (11.4 cm) in overall length, it is the largest of the three forms. Olive green when adult, it is somewhat duller when young. The dwarf Budgett's frog is known scientifically as *L. llanensis* (the specific name refers to the pampas-like *llanos*, the habitat of the frog). The smallest of the three, it is adult at about 2.5 inches (6.2 cm) in length. The hybrid, once known as *L. asper*, is of intermediate size. Although those first imported from Argentina were marketed as Budgett's frogs, their aggressive attitudes have now won them the moniker of "Freddie Kruger frogs" (and we thought the marketing name of

The Budgett's frog, Lepidobatrachus laevis, *is rather regularly available. It is a relative of the horned frogs.*

"Pac-Man" for the various horned frogs was bad!).

The Chacoan Burrowing Frog

Chacophrys pierotti, is the last of the ceratophrines seen with any regularity. Attractively colored in greens and browns, it is adult at about 2.5 inches (6.2 cm) in length. It too is an aggressive, big-headed species, that is now being bred in reasonable numbers. This species, quite similar to the horned frogs in appearance and every bit as cannibalistic, is indigenous to Argentina's Gran Chaco region.

Care of Captive Ceratophrines

(Also see chapters on health and terrarium construction, pages 16 and 32.)

General guidelines: Horned frogs and their relatives, including *Lepidobatrachus,* can be cannibalistic and can consume remarkably large prey items. Juveniles are especially predacious: always keep juvenile specimens separated from each other. It is somewhat safer to keep adult specimens communally. Do not mix species. If you opt for a community situation, make certain that all specimens are well fed and of similar size.

Although the *ceratophrines* currently on the market are rather easily kept, there are a few things you should do to ensure their health and well-being. Always buy captive-bred and -hatched specimens when available, to make certain that the health of your new pet has not been compromised by the rigors of collection from the wild, adverse holding conditions, or a high level of parasitism. Captive-bred and -hatched leptodactylids, even the more difficult-to-keep species such as the Surinam horned frog, are more likely to accept the insects, fishes, and rodents that we traditionally offer them for food.

Diet: As new metamorphs, horned frogs may be fed small fish or crickets or both, lightly dusted with a powdered

Chacophrys pierrotti is a small, voracious horned frog relative. It has only recently been captive bred.

vitamin/mineral supplement. Since the frogs' growth is rapid, the supplements are particularly important in preventing metabolic bone disease, which is an actual softening and demineralization of the bones. With the growth of the frog, larger food items can be offered, depending on the species. Fully grown female ornate horned and chaco frogs can easily overcome and swallow an adult breeder-sized mouse, while adult males of these species may be fed average-sized "pet-store" mice (about three-quarters grown).

Despite their inactivity, horned frogs, especially the younger specimens, require a fair amount of food. New metamorphs will need a suitably sized guppy, a tiny goldfish, or a couple of small crickets at least every second day. Daily feeding is probably better yet. Both the size of the food items and the duration between feedings can be increased with the growth of your frog. Adult ornate horned frogs

will not need to eat more than once a week. Although they will not need as much vitamin/mineral supplement as the smaller frogs, it is still a good idea to supply these additives at least once every two weeks.

Horned frogs and their kin are voracious feeders. When attempting to catch live, unrestrained rodents or insects, the frogs often ingest fair amounts of their substrate. Fatal impactions are far from rare. Two things can be done to reduce the possibility of intestinal impactions: 1. Feed your frog with forceps. Bringing the food directly to the frog will dramatically lessen the chance of its ingesting gravel, dirt, and plants. 2. Use care in choosing the substrate (if any) for your frog's container.

Caging: Many keepers have found it easiest to slope a suitably sized aquarium containing nothing but a little water in the low end. Though lacking aesthetic appeal, this severely simple arrangement has the advantage of being wonderfully easy to clean. It attests to the adaptability of these frogs, which will survive for many years in such Spartan settings. A setup nearly as austere requires a section of sturdy, flat sponge cut to fit tightly into about half the tank bottom. The tank can then be kept level, and the frog will sit atop the sponge when it wishes to get out of the water. From these two simplified terrariums, the setups can range through increasingly complicated designs to a planted woodland terrarium that is stunning but difficult to maintain properly. A compromise between the two extremes is quite likely the best.

Such an intermediate design might be a terrarium with a substrate of small (pea-sized) river rock. (We prefer smooth river rock to rough silica aquarium gravel; if accidentally ingested by the frog, rock is passed more easily.) A shallow, water-filled plastic or glass bowl big enough for the frog to sit in easily, should be sunk nearly to its rim in the gravel. A sturdy potted plant, such as a Chinese ever-

green (*Aglaonema*) or dumb-cane (*Dieffenbachia*), can be used as a decoration if the enclosure is large enough.

The necessity of absolute cleanliness in the terrarium cannot be overemphasized. Amphibians retain the necessary level of body moisture by almost constantly absorbing water through the skin, as well as taking it in through the cloaca. If the moist surfaces with which the animals are in contact are allowed to foul, the bacteria-laden water absorbed will soon cause disease. Water dishes should be cleaned at least every second day (more often if the water is obviously fouled) and the gravel should be thoroughly washed weekly. Our preference is to keep an extra supply of washed and sterilized gravel on hand. We change the gravel weekly (or as necessary), removing that in the terrarium and replacing it with an equal amount of clean gravel. The removed gravel is then washed and sterilized (we use a weak Clorox solution), then thoroughly washed again. It is then ready for the next change.

Backyard Favorites and Exotic Rarities: Family Bufonidae

Throughout the years, most toads have caught the eyes of youngsters rather than herpetoculturists. The latter often concentrate their efforts on brightly colored species with immediate sales value, provided breeding efforts are successful. Youngsters, on the other hand, require no economic incentive to channel their interests. To them, as to us long ago, a toad is one of the most wondrous of creatures. Even today, after over five decades, we seldom fail to stop and admire each and every toad we see.

The "Arboreal" Toads

Most toads are ground-dwelling species. A very few have arboreal tendencies. Most of the "arboreal" toads are small in size. One, however, the Malayan climbing toad (*Pedostibes hosei*), is about 3½ inches (8.9 cm) long and rather prettily colored, with orange tubercles and spots against an olive or black ground. This toad would be most comfortable in a terrarium setup similar to that used for treefrogs. *Pedostibes* is only occasionally available in the pet trade; if in good condition when received (many are not), it usually proves hardy and rather long-lived.

The Ground-dwelling Toads

For the most part, toads are immediately recognizable as toads. They are rather squat, variably warty, and often have a dry-appearing skin. Their protuberant eyes display wonderfully intricate designs of gold in the irides (irises). Many toads have prominent parotoid (shoulder) glands that produce an acrid-tasting toxin (trust us on this—do not taste the exudate yourself). The exudate is effective in deterring some predators, but of little consequence to others.

Toads generally seek water only for the purpose of breeding, although some are rather extensively aquatic, seldom wandering far from the environs of ponds, rivers, or other water sources. Sixteen species occur in the United States and southern Canada, and many others join the ranks as you travel southward through Latin America. In fact, toads occur on most continents. Many, when seen in pet shops, can be difficult to identify. Even to try you'll need to know where the toad is from; and then you'll need some time with the appropriate field guides. Often you will wind up with two or three possibilities, and the final "identification" will be little more than an educated guess.

Toads of the United States

In the United States toads range in size from the 1-inch-long (2.5 cm) oak toad, *Bufo quercicus*, of the southeast, which vocalizes in chicklike peeps, to the 8-inch-long (20.3 cm) giant toad, *Bufo marinus*, native to the lower Rio Grande Valley of Texas. Giant toads

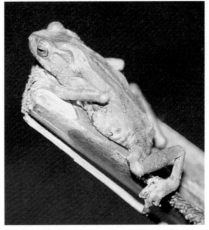

Males of the strange little Malayan climbing toad, Pedostibes hosei, *are less colorful and slightly smaller than most females.*

The giant toad, Bufo marinus. *Its toxins are complex and virulent.*

are frequently sold in the pet trade, and they are now a firmly established alien species in peninsular Florida, Australia, and the West Indies. (They were deliberately introduced in Australia and may well have been intentionally released in Florida's sugarcane fields. How they became

established in the West Indies is unknown.) This big, brown, heavily tubercled toad has tremendous parotoid glands, which produce an extremely virulent toxin, sometimes in copious quantities. Dogs, cats, and foxes that have grasped and injured this species have been known to die

The American toad, Bufo americanus, *ranges widely over much of eastern North America. All toads are often referred to as "hop-toads."*

The American green toad, Bufo debilis *ssp., is a small and beautiful species.*

When printed, the name Melanophryniscus stelzneri *is greater in length than the toad itself. The common name currently attached to this species is "Argentine flame-bellied toadlet."*

as a result of their indiscretion. Although no human fatalities have been noted, it would be wise to wash your hands thoroughly after handling this, or any other big toad species.

Giant toads not only eat typical live fare (large insects, arachnids, small rodents, and the like) but are among the very few terrestrial anurans known to eat prepared foods. It is not unusual in urban Miami to see several of these big creatures hunched over "Rover's" feed bowl, eating chunks of dog food.

Two of the prettiest species native to the United States are the Sonoran and the common green toads, *Bufo retiformis* and *B. debilis* ssp. Both approach 2 inches (5 cm) in size and have a rather flattened body. Both live in irrigated regions and oases in the deserts of the Southwest. Both are very hardy, readily accepting suitable sized insects and arachnids. The Sonoran green toad, a protected species, now is seldom seen captive in collections other than those of zoos. The common green toad, which has an eastern and a western subspecies, remains quite common and may occasionally be purchased rather inexpensively. Both species have nasal, insectlike trills with fair carrying power and may be found actively breeding during the desert monsoons.

Green toads (and most other "typical" toads) thrive in spacious terrariums with sandy loam substrates kept just on the damp side of dry. Most will readily utilize a shallow water bowl for additional moisture requirements. Be sure to clean the water bowl promptly when it is dirtied and periodically replace the

The colorful venter of Melanophryniscus stelzneri *is clearly shown in this photograph.*

Harlequin frogs are difficult to keep. The golden harlequin frog, Atelopus flavescens, *is the species most commonly available to hobbyists.*

substrate. We keep our green toads with about 3 inches (7.6 cm) of soil, and for the most part they remain burrowed. Nocturnal in their activity patterns, they will be induced by occasional heavy misting to emerge and forage for their insect repast. They seem to be long-lived little creatures. We have had some, adult when received, for more than four years. We are not aware of captive breeding programs for either species.

Argentine Flame-bellied Toad

A very pretty little Argentine toad currently available in the pet trade in the United States is the Argentine flame-bellied toadlet, *Melanophryniscus stelzneri*. Only 1 inch (2.5 cm) in length, this tiny creature seems quite temperature-tolerant and hardy. The flame-bellied toadlet has a few bright yellow spots on an otherwise jet black dorsum, and a black-reticulated, flame-red venter. Our specimens are active by day and perform gymnastics on plant leaves with some agility. They feed avidly on termites, aphids, small, innocuous ant species, and—if they are really hungry—pinhead-sized crickets. The toads frequently sit at the edge of the water in their large (50 gallon or approximately 20 L) terrarium, but we seldom see them actually enter the watery world. When they do so, they swim rather well, but jerkily, and soon return to land. We have had a half dozen for more than a year, but although the little males frequently have voiced their soft, high-pitched peeps, we have seen no eggs or tadpoles.

Harlequin Frogs

Not all Bufonidae are warmth-loving, low-altitude species. One exception is the harlequin frog, *Atelopus* spp. This neotropical frog usually is associated with clear, bubbling cloud-forest streams. Many populations are now in decline while others seem stable, despite moderate collecting from them. Yet others—some in virtually undisturbed habitat—have disappeared entirely, becoming frightening statistics in the perplexing mystery of the "vanishing frogs."

Appearance: The harlequin frogs are, for the most part, brightly colored. They are on the small side, with a snout-to-vent length of about 2 inches (5.1 cm). Most have an angular, gangly appearance. Some species from chill mountaintop habitats are more compact and shorter-legged.

The species most often available in the American pet trade is *A. flavescens,* a form that, like most other harlequin frogs, lacks a common name. *Flavescens*, one of the slender, angular forms, can be either pretty or dull. Many specimens have a yellow(ish) dorsum and a lavender venter; others may add to this color scheme a liberal amount of red lateral flecking; still others may be an overall yellowish-gray, both dorsally and ventrally, and not particularly pretty.

Color variation, even within some populations, is great. In fact, one of the most confusing, variable, and aptly named Central American species is *Atelopus varius.* While in Costa Rica we saw in the same mountain stream *varius* that were black on yellow, yellow on black, yellow on turquoise, red and yellow on black, black on chartreuse, cobalt on yellow, and more. Some color combinations produced a rather dull frog; others were as gaudy as—or even flashier than—the bright arrow-poison frogs. All were wonderful, and we spent hours frog-watching as the little *Atelopus* clambered about in and on the shores of that stream. Most were perched alertly on mossy, emergent rocks.

Habitat: On subsequent trips to other areas of the neotropics, we found such rocky streams to be the favored habitats of many species of harlequin frogs. When the habitats of some species were largely devoid of rocks, the harlequin frogs utilized fallen limbs, trunks, and stream edges as their vantage points. The males of the species we saw were quite territorial, avidly grappling with other males that intruded into their territory.

Diet: Harlequin frogs are avid feeders on small mealworms, butterworms and waxworms, small crickets, sowbugs, termites, and field plankton.

Like many other amphibians that are bedecked in aposematic colors (brilliant hues indicating special defensive capabilities), harlequin frogs are both toxic and diurnal. The toxins produced in the skins of the harlequin frogs vary from rather benign to quite virulent. It is not known whether, as in the case of arrow-poison frogs, a short period of captivity will diminish the virulency of the toxins produced by a given frog. However, if the virulency of the skin secretions is dependent on the ingestion of certain insects found in the wild, it seems likely that the toxins of harlequin frogs fed on a diet of crickets, sow bugs, and waxworms will soon lose their potency.

Caging: Harlequin frogs' reputation as "delicate" pets is not without basis. Before reaching the specialized dealers who can care for them adequately, many of the imported harlequin frogs have been subjected to intolerable warmth, crowding, and unclean conditions. Many are seriously debilitated long before the hobbyist has an opportunity to acquire them. These frogs often succumb quickly to bacterial disease or other problems, no matter how lavish the captive care and facilities provided them.

However, if the specimens with which you start are fresh and healthy,

harlequin frogs can be maintained in captivity. Remember that these frogs require coolness and cleanliness. Nighttime air temperatures of 55 to 58°F (13–15°C) and daytime highs of 66 to 70°F (18–21°C) are ideal. Water temperatures can vary somewhat less, from 62 to 69°F (16–20°C). The need for cleanliness cannot be overemphasized!

The terrarium for most *Atelopus* will be an easily made refinement of the semiaquatic terrarium; we call it the stream terrarium. It requires a long tank. The minimum size is 20 gallons (75 L), and 50 (200 L) would be better. The few items needed for construction are readily available: a profusion of large, smoothly rounded river rocks, a few pounds of pea-sized river rock, a small, sturdy plastic tray (for the land area), materials for the land area (a little pea-sized gravel), a vine, a little potting soil, a few dead leaves (optional), and a powerhead fitted to a filter sponge. Place the large rocks lengthwise along both sides of the tank, leaving a channel in the center. Place the filter sponge/powerhead at one end of the tank, secure the plastic tray containing the land area above the powerhead, and add dechlorinated water. Put in a mossy log for decoration if you choose, add the frogs and lighting, and presto—a stream terrarium.

Breeding: All harlequin frogs are difficult to keep. To our knowledge, none have been bred in captivity.

Note: Harlequin frogs are species suitable only for experienced keepers committed to attaining viable, self-sustaining captive populations. Continued pressure on wild populations by the pet trade should be discouraged.

Neotropical Forestland Gems: Family Dendrobatidae

The Arrow-poison Frogs

Although the sales of some tree-frogs and horned frogs probably exceed those of arrow-poison frogs in volume, it is the latter that have the greatest number of "hard-core" devotees. Anyone familiar with the beauty and reproductive intricacies of the various neotropical arrow-poison frogs can certainly understand why so many hobbyists show enthusiasm for this group of anurans.

One reason for the popularity of arrow-poison frogs probably is their beauty: they are very brightly colored and patterned. Another reason may

The reticulated arrow-poison frog, Dendrobates reticulatus, *is another beautiful species that is rather infrequently seen in herpetoculture.*

be their unusual history: these frogs' toxins have long been employed to poison the tips of arrows used in hunting by the native peoples of Central and South America. Most of the poisonous skin exudates must be processed to maximize their toxicity. Some are toxic "as is." A third reason may be the fascinating patterns of care given eggs and young by the caretaking parent.

Genera

Until rather recently, the poisonous members of the Dendrobatidae that wore "advertisement colors" were contained within two genera, *Dendrobates* and *Phyllobates*. Today, however, two additional genera have been added, *Epipedobates* and *Minyobates*.

Besides these four genera of poisonous species, there are two basically nonpoisonous genera in the family: *Colostethus*, the rocket frogs, and *Aromobates*, the highly odoriferous skunk frog. Although there are more species in the nonpoisonous genera (more than 100 rocket frogs and the single skunk frog) than in the poisonous ones (65 species), they are seldom available to the hobbyist. Nor is it likely they would find favor with many hobbyists if they were available.

Appearance: Arrow-poison frogs are not large. Those commonly found in the pet trade are small, with a snout-to-vent length of ¾ to 2 inches

A strawberry frog that lives up to its name.

The pink leopard phase of Dendrobates pumilio.

The common name of strawberry arrow-poison frog is not always accurate for *Dendrobates pumilio.* As we can see, this species may vary in ground color from intense red, through pink, to green and blue.

(1.9–5.1 cm). These are often very common within restricted areas, and are now protected by the Commission on International Trade in Endangered Species (CITES).

Color: If it is brilliance of color that interests you, you can't go wrong

here. Arrow-poison frogs come in greens, blacks, yellows, reds, oranges, blues, and combinations of those colors. Not all populations of a given species are colored similarly. In the strawberry frog, *Dendrobates pumilio,* for instance, there are many

A green morph with touches of bronze on its back and legs.

A black-legged Costa Rican morph of Dendrobates pumilio.

color morphs: red frogs with blue legs, red frogs with black legs, green frogs with black reticulation, red frogs with white reticulation, and even some that are gray on blue. This variety of colors demonstrates how inappropriate a common name (strawberry frog) can be. This species is not the only one to display such marked diversity of color; in fact, among the poisonous members of this family, color variation within the species seems more the norm than the exception.

Toxicity: How toxic are the arrow-poison frogs? In nature their toxicity varies by species and perhaps by population. Some of the less brilliantly colored species seem to have little toxicity, while some of the more brilliantly colored species are dangerously toxic.

It would appear that the title "most toxic of all" is shared about equally by three closely related species of the genus *Phyllobates.* Denizens of southwestern Colombia, these three are the golden, *P. terribilis*, the bicolored, *P. bicolor,* and the gold-banded, *P. aurotaenia*, arrow-poison frogs. None of the three are common in America, but they are popular in Europe. All, though pretty, are a rather unspectacular golden color or gold and black (or black and gold). The toxicity of these three frogs in nature is so great that it would be necessary only to rub an arrow tip on the skin of an upset adult frog to gather sufficient toxin to kill most prey.

The most toxic of the skin secretions of other arrow-poison frogs are exuded only when the frog is seriously or mortally injured. To obtain the lethal arrow-poisons from these frogs, their captors put them to death. For even greater efficacy, the poisons are often mixed with others from different sources.

Interestingly, even the most toxic of the arrow-poison frogs seem (and we emphasize "seem") to lose most or all of their toxic properties after varying periods of captivity. This effect, most noticeable in frogs several generations removed from the wild, indicates that certain conditions of the natural habitat (obviously) are not duplicated exactly in captivity. Two of the most evident variables are the insects consumed as food by the frogs and the chemical contents of the substrates. Since it is known that, in the wild, arrow-poison frogs eat large numbers of various ant species (they are *myrmecophageous*) and immense numbers of other forest insects), perhaps the foods abet the continued manufacture of the frog's skin toxins. Neither the native ants nor the other native insects are available to captives. Nor can soil components be duplicated. Perhaps the lack of one or all of these accounts for the more benign skin secretions of long-term captive frogs.

Whether newly imported or long-term captives, arrow-poison frogs should be handled with extreme care, for the sake of both the handled and the handler. Unfrightened frogs are less apt to exude toxins than frightened ones. Long-term captives exude fewer secretions than new imports. The three species of dangerously toxic *Phyllobates* should never be free-handed (touched with bare hands). Move them with nets or by inducing them to hop into a jar or glass used only for that purpose. The skin toxins of the frogs can enter the bloodstream of a handler through abrasions or, it is thought, through the pores. It is not smart to take chances.

Behavior: Aggression and territoriality go hand in hand in many reproductively active frog species, but these responses are nowhere more manifest than in the arrow-poison frogs. Males grapple with males of like (and sometimes unlike) species, females grapple with females, satellite males sneak in and out until found and evicted. Exact responses differ from species to species, but when these frogs are confined to the small space of a terrarium there can be serious—even tragic—consequences. Only males that hold territory can successfully breed, and to attain and retain that right they will mercilessly bully (or even kill) rivals. Subordinate specimens are apt to be so severely stressed that normal feeding is precluded.

Breeding: Arrow-poison frogs typically display reproductive characteristics unknown elsewhere in the frog world (except, perhaps, in the look-alike mantellas of Madagascar). Precise patterns of parental care are shown by most arrow-poison frogs. In some species it is the male that provides the care, in other species the female. The challenge of simulating in a terrarium the environmental conditions necessary to induce breeding behavior in these frogs is accepted by many herpeticulturists. Reproduction and parental care of the tadpoles are carried out in several ways.

Most arrow-poison frogs do not indulge in amplexus. The males of some species may sit on the backs of the females, but this usually happens prior to, not during, the expelling of the eggs. The frogs do indulge in much tactile stimulation, stroking each other's back, sides, and cloacal areas with their foretoes.

The actual fertilization of the eggs is accomplished in several ways. The males of some species may first expel sperm onto a chosen deposition site, after which the female lays her eggs on that spot. In other cases there may be vent-to-vent contact while the frogs are facing in opposite directions. Several minutes may pass between egg laying and fertilization, with the male sometimes leaving the site, then returning to fertilize the eggs.

The females of a few species, notably *D. pumilio, D. histrionicus, D.*

granuliferus, and *D. speciosus,* lay fertile eggs, either on fallen leaves or in bromeliad cups. If on the ground, the female remains near the egg mass, leaving only for brief periods to feed and find water. When the young hatch, she carries them to the bromeliad cups. After depositing them, she then returns periodically to deposit infertile "food eggs" in each bromeliad cup for the tadpoles to feed on. In captive programs, dilute yolk of hen egg (uncooked) has also been offered with varying success to these specialized feeders.

A specially designed terrarium will be necessary. For egg-laying, these species need a vertically oriented enclosure in which small, spineless bromeliad types (Vresia, etc.) grow.

Although female arrow-poison frogs of the reticulatus complex (*D. fantasticus, D. ventrimaculatus, D. quinquevittatus, D. reticulatus,* and others) seem to deposit food eggs for their tadpoles, hobbyists question whether these are actually critical to development. If provided, food eggs may result in stronger tadpoles, but the larvae of some species have been brought through to metamorphosis on prepared foods alone.

The more typical method of reproduction involves the laying of the eggs in terrestrial situations by the female and their subsequent fertilization by the male. The male waits nearby until the eggs hatch. After hatching, the tadpoles wriggle onto the back of the male, who carries them from the terrestrial deposition site to the chosen waterhole, where the tadpoles then undergo normal growth and metamorphosis. This rather standard method of parental care is utilized by most species of arrow-poison frogs commonly seen in captivity. Some examples are *D. tinctorius, D. auratus, Epipedobates tricolor,* and *Phyllobates vittatus.*

Although the pattern may vary, the pretty little Dendrobates leucomelas *is always clad in black and yellow.*

Of the arrow-poison frogs, the green and black Dendrobates auratus *is one of the hardier and more easily bred species.*

Species Accounts

The strawberry frog, *Dendrobates pumilio*, occurs in the Gulf drainage from Nicaragua east to central Panama. It is one of the smallest and most beautiful of the species commonly seen in the pet trade. Strawberry frogs are specialized

breeders that lay very small egg clutches. Parental care is extensive, and once hatched the young have an excellent chance of survival.

The black and yellow arrow-poison frog, *D. leucomelas*, is one of our favorite species. This beautiful anuran is fairly large (to 1.5 inches or

Spectacular in both appearance and price, the blue arrow-poison frog, Dendrobates azureus *is only today becoming more readily available to hobbyists.*

The harlequin arrow-poison frog, Dendrobates histrionicus, *is very variable in color and considered a difficult species to maintain.*

Although some morphs of Dendrobates tinctorius *are clad in pastels, most specimens seen in the pet trade are brilliant yellow and bright blue. This is one of the more commonly seen species.*

3.8 cm), hardy, a nonspecialized breeder, and probably better known to herpetoculturists than to field researchers. About six eggs are usually laid in each clutch. This species is of rather standardized color, being yellow-orange banded with inky black. In occasional specimens some of the bands are broken into spots. Even more rarely, the bands are replaced by haphazardly placed spots. The primary range of this species is Venezuela and eastern Guyana.

The green and black arrow-poison frog is also called the golden arrow-poison frog, from the Latin

The Phantasmal arrow-poison frog, Epipedobates tricolor, *is now commonly seen in captivity.*

Orange stripes and metallic blue-green legs typify Phyllobates vittatus. *It is commonly called the Golfodulcean arrow-poison frog.*

69

species name: *D. auratus*. It is the most frequently seen and easily bred of the arrow-poison frogs. Although this beautiful anuran is usually velvety green with black spots or bands, specimens with ground colors of cobalt blue, turquoise, gold-green or nearly entirely black are occasionally seen. This frog, which attains a snout-to-vent length of about 1.5 inches (3.8 cm), is a nonspecialized breeder that deposits small egg clutches. Eggs number from four to 10 per clutch. The frog remains abundant in suitable habitat from Costa Rica to extreme western Colombia. It has also been introduced in Hawaii.

The blue arrow-poison frog, *D. azureus,* is one of the most coveted members of the genus. A fairly large species (to about 1.75 inches or 4.4 cm), it is restricted to Surinam in distribution. From two to 10 eggs are laid, and both sexes are known to transport the hatched tadpoles to water. Although they are not difficult to breed, there are comparatively few specimens in captivity. Very successful breeding programs are in place at Chaffee Zoological Gardens in Fresno, California, and in Texas at the Fort Worth Zoo. The National Aquarium in Baltimore, Maryland, is also working with the species. The bright blue ground color is variably patterned with dots and dashes dorsally. These dark spots are less profuse laterally and virtually nonexistent posterioventrally.

The harlequin arrow-poison frog, *Dendrobates histrionicus,* comes in a bewildering array of colors and patterns. The term "variable" truly fits this frog. Colors include gray-reticulated yellow (often with an orange tinge to the frog's head), olive brown, brilliant orange-red, pale green, and butter yellow. One interesting morph, usually of olive-brown to jet-black ground color with a big red spot on the dorsum, is termed the "bull's-eye morph" by hobbyists. Others may be entirely brown on the dorsum with a broad red stripe on the venter.

This is one of the more demanding and difficult species to breed, but if kept clean and cool it can be maintained. This frog comes from the Pacific drainages of Colombia and Ecuador.

The blue and yellow arrow-poison frog, *D. tinctorius,* another variable species, is closely allied to the blue arrow-poison frog. The name blue and yellow is often accurate, but the species also occurs in yellow and black, white and black, white and blue, and blue and black. This species ranges over much of the three Guyanas. Also known as the dyeing arrow-poison frog, it was once used in dyeing native textiles. The frog is easily maintained, easily bred, and at a snout-to-vent length of 2 inches (5.1 cm), it is one of the largest members of the genus. Clutches average about nine eggs.

The Phantasmal arrow-poison frog, *E. tricolor,* is another variable and pretty species. This is a small frog: Adults seldom attain lengths in excess of 1 inch (2.5 cm). This longitudinally banded species is often clad in a ground color of russet to rose with yellow, tan, green, blue, or cream-colored stripes of variable width. In some specimens the light bands converge and dominate the color scheme. Coral-red to vermilion flash markings are often present on the posterior surface of the thigh. Although small, this frog produces many more eggs per clutch than is the norm among arrow-poison frogs. Fifteen eggs per clutch is common, 35 have been recorded.

This arrow-poison frog is hardy and easily bred. Its range extends southward from south central Ecuador to extreme northwestern Peru.

The Golfodulcean arrow-poison frog, *P. vittatus,* although found in only a tiny area of Pacific eastern Costa Rica, is well represented in captive collections. A generalized breeder, this orange-striped 1-inch-long (2.5 cm) forest gem produces up to 20 eggs. The ground color of the dorsum is black, that of the venter black-mottled green or gray.

Captive Care for All Arrow-poison Frogs

Diet: Small though they may be, arrow-poison frogs eat a lot. Their appetites are nearly insatiable. Providing an adequate and continuous supply of their favorite foods is often the most difficult aspect of successfully maintaining and breeding these frogs. The type and size of the feed insects will be dictated by the type and size of the arrow-poison frog being fed. Fortunately, pinhead-sized crickets are now commercially available from many bait supply dealers. These will keep your frogs from starving during lean times. However, most arrow-poison frogs are not overly fond of domestically raised crickets. (At least ours aren't!) So, while we do have crickets on hand and keep a few in the terrarium with the frogs at most times, the anurans' main diet consists of termites, springtails, and suitably sized field plankton. Vestigial-winged fruit flies are often presented as treats. When aphids infest our trees and shrubs we shake many of these insects into the arrow-poison frog cages. The little anurans truly seem to enjoy them. Of all the insects offered, however, the termites and fruit flies appeal most to the arrow-poison frogs. We supply them in as great a quantity as possible.

If you are interested in breeding your arrow-poison frogs (and we hope you are), you will find the new metamorphs of some of the smaller species so tiny that even fruit flies are an oversized meal. For these, spring-tails, the tiniest of aphids, newly born crickets, and the smallest of the field plankton must be provided.

The most common and persistent malady to plague captive colonies of arrow-poison frogs of all species is malformation of the forelimbs. Termed "spindly-leg syndrome," this is thought to be a diet-related problem. It is not known with certainty when the problem originates. Some hobbyists believe the nutritional deficiencies start with the female frog prior to egg laying; others think that it is the tadpoles that are fed improperly. Certainly all possibilities must be considered. Feed all frogs—especially breeding ones—highly nutritious diets augmented with vitamin D_3 and calcium. Feed the tadpoles well and often. And to expand the net of safety, closely monitor and maintain both water quality and suggested temperature parameters.

Caging: Arrow-poison frogs are creatures of tropical rainforests. Although their habitats may adjoin forest streams, the frogs seldom enter water other than quiet pools and backwaters, and that they do with relative infrequency. It would seem that some captive specimens enter water solely to accomplish the release of their tadpoles.

High relative humidity, warmth, visual barriers, and ample food are required to successfully maintain arrow-poison frogs. Even when these prerequisites are met, some species can prove difficult captives and some nearly impossible to breed. Arrow-poison frogs that were themselves captive-bred reproduce easiest in captivity.

A heavily planted woodland or rainforest terrarium will help your captives thrive. For a colony of eight to 10 frogs we suggest a terrarium of no less than 50 gallons (200 L) in size. For basic construction suggestions see page 17. There are some special

The beautiful little Phantasmal arrow-poison frog, Epipedobates tricolor, *is of variable color. (Also see photos on pages 69 and 73.)*

considerations for arrow-poison frogs, which are extremely territorial. It is essential that their terrarium be provided with many visual barriers. Even then, the condition of all members of the colony or breeding group has to be frequently and carefully monitored. Plants, plants, and more plants, in addition to other hiding areas and very shallow water receptacles, are suggested here. Philodendrons, epipremnums, piper, fittonia, maranta, and other moisture/heat-tolerant tropical plants are good choices.

To grow live plants—even shade-tolerant jungle plants—strong overhead lighting is essential. Without sufficient lighting the plants will become leggy and incapable of photosynthesis, and they will die within a short time.

Arrow-poison frogs have well-developed finger and toe discs that allow them to climb nearly as adeptly as treefrogs. The terrarium must be tightly closed to prevent escape. A screen top will prevent the escape of the frogs while providing for humidity regulation. During cool or dry weather, lay a sheet of plexiglass or glass over most or all of the screen top. Slide the solid cover back as far as necessary to lower the humidity, or close it more tightly to increase humidity.

Besides the plants, several small, opaque plastic or coconut-shell huts will be necessary. We prefer the coconuts. It is the shell of the coconut, not the fibrous outer husk, that must be used. Cut the shell in half, remove the white meat, cut entryways, and place the halves open side down atop the substrate. Shallow water dishes (petri dishes or ashtrays) should be placed within view of each hut.

Temperatures between 73°F (23°C) at night and 82°F (27°C) in the daytime are ideal for most arrow-poison frogs.

Caution: Some of these wonderful little frogs can be rather easily maintained—at least as adults—in captivity; many can even be rather easily bred. Before acquiring any, though, be absolutely certain that you have food sources firmly in line. Do not depend on baby crickets alone to feed your arrow-poison frogs. Be certain to add D_3 and calcium to the diets of your frogs. These additives are especially important to babies that are rapidly growing.

Don't crowd, overcool, or otherwise stress your specimens. If you follow these suggestions, we believe you will find the larger and hardier of the arrow-poison frogs interesting, enjoyable, and well worth your efforts.

Many hobbyists are attracted by the color variability offered by Phantasmal arrow-poison frogs.

Arboreal Favorites: Family Hylidae

Many different hylid frogs are kept by both casual hobbyists and experienced herpetoculturists. We look here at some of the favorites.

Red-eyed Treefrogs

The red-eyed treefrog (*Agalychnis callidryas*) is a beautiful phyllomedusine hylid that occurs over much of Mexico and Central America. Although it has been imported periodically in large numbers, it was only recently that efforts at captive breeding of the red-eyed treefrogs succeeded.

The taxonomic status of the red-eye is uncertain. Although to many observers these red-eyed, blue-flanked anurans may seem the same throughout their range, there are several rather consistent differences. It is possible that three or more sibling species are masquerading under a single name. This question will eventually be sorted out by geneticists. If *A. callidryas* is a species complex rather than a single species, that might help to explain the inviability (egg-death, malformations, and death at metamorphosis) that has been noted by several potential breeders. On the other hand, if only a single species is involved, we have to look elsewhere for the causes of the problem.

If you decide to try breeding this species, it would probably be good to get all your specimens at the same time, from a single dealer. That would more or less assure you that they had been collected from the same general area and increase the chance of their being genetically compatible.

Appearance: The red-eyed treefrog is one of the world's most beautiful tailless amphibians. Females, the larger sex, attain a length of only about 3 inches (7.6 cm). Males reach a snout-to-vent length (SVL) of about 2¼ inches (5.7 cm). What red-eyes lack in size, they make up for in coloration.

Color: The body color of red-eyed treefrogs is variable. Distressed treefrogs (and, more rarely, contented ones) may be some shade of brown. More usually, though, the body color is on the chartreuse side of leaf green. White dorsal spots may be profuse, few, or lacking entirely. The amount of blue on the flanks can vary considerably from population to population. In the frogs most extensively marked, the blue can begin at and involve the apices of the forelimbs, continue on the upper arm itself, then extend to the groin and upper femur. The blue may range from robin's egg blue through sky blue to deep purplish blue. Sometimes the shading on the sides is brown instead of blue. The white barring on the blue flanks can be even more variable. The vertical sections may be narrowly spaced, widely spaced, thick, or thin. They may be connected at top or bottom or both by horizontal white markings. Some of the variability seems to be related to the geographic location from which the frogs come; some seems individual. The venter, underlimbs, and toes are suffused with a variable amount of golden yellow.

Sexing: Red-eyed treefrogs are not always easily sexed, and perhaps the simplest method is to listen to their vocalizations: only the males vocalize. Most adult females are larger than adult males. Males develop horny, dark nuptial excrescences on their thumbs when reproductively active.

Behavior: For most of each day, the red-eyed treefrog sits quietly, eyes closed, legs drawn tightly against its body. It looks like a green burl, a nodule—almost anything except a frog. In the evening, however, especially if the terrarium is liberally misted at dusk, the red-eye "comes to life." It is then that the angular grace of the treefrog can be appreciated and that its color is at its brightest. The limbs are long and slender, the gaze of the ruby-red eyes is alert and almost quizzical.

Although they are fully capable of leaping (sometimes prodigiously), as often as not red-eyed treefrogs progress in a hand-over-hand, foot-over-foot walking movement. The opposable toes grasp leaves and limbs securely and tightly, providing ample dexterity for this frog species' active life in the trees.

Diet: Red-eyed treefrogs are insectivorous and avidly consume all manner of small, fast-moving invertebrates. Captives do well on crickets, flies, and, if available, suitable field plankton. If field plankton is used, be certain that you net the insects in areas where insecticides have not been applied. Although red-eyed treefrogs may be reluctant to hunt slow-moving insects like waxworms and small sizes of giant mealworms, they may often accept these foods if held out in forceps.

If you provide a great amount of freshly collected field plankton, most of the vitamins and minerals the frogs need will be supplied by the insects. However, if you are among the many who depend largely upon commercially raised crickets for your amphib-

ians' food source, vitamin D_3 and calcium levels will need to be augmented. Although several finely powdered vitamin D_3 and calcium compounds for reptiles and amphibians are now available in most pet shops, we continue to use the more broadly based Osteoform, a product of Vet-A-Mix, Inc. We have found it an entirely satisfactory supplement.

Caging: Since red-eyes are an active species, we suggest a terrarium of at least 20-gallon (75 L) size for a pair. A 50-gallon (200 L) or larger tank is preferable, if budget and space allow.

A forest species, red-eyed treefrogs prefer lushly planted terrariums in which high relative humidity is maintained. Proper ventilation is also essential, however. Both ventilation and humidity can be regulated by covering a greater or lesser amount of the screen top with glass or plastic. Do not keep the tank so humid that droplets of water form and run down the sides. A slight haze of moisture on the glass is more acceptable, especially when you want to stimulate breeding behavior. Continued high relative humidity and misting induce both normal activity patterns and reproductive behavior in red-eyes, especially if the misting occurs at dusk.

Since we favor the use of live plants in terrariums, we suggest such species as philodendrons and epipremnums (a well-known member of the latter genus is the beautifully variegated plant sold as "pothos"), small anthurium cultivars, spathiphyllum (often called peace lily), the various marantas (prayer-plants), and other commonly grown foliage species. Small, spineless air plants (bromeliads) are also terrarium favorites. Depending on how your terrarium is set up and whether the plants are well adapted for your particular setup, the plants may need

The red-eyed treefrog, Agalychnis cal-lidryas, *is one of the most beautiful and coveted of hylid frogs.*

frequent replacing or may be very long-lived. For specifics regarding the construction of semiaquatic and woodland terrariums, see page 19.

In the warmth and humidity of southwest Florida we have kept red-eyed tree frogs outdoors in wire-covered wood-frame cages in all but the coldest weather. Temperatures below 50°F (10°C) and above 90°F (34°C) were survived with equanimity. These frogs are also ideal candidates for communal breeding in a temperature-controlled greenhouse.

Breeding: Red-eyed treefrogs are neotropical leaf frogs. In the wild, the females deposit their egg clusters on leaves or lianas overhanging the water. The arboreal egg masses are contained within a gelatinous outer coating, rather than the foam nest so often associated with this type of egg-laying. The tensile strength of the

coating deteriorates over time and finally the hatchling tadpoles wriggle free, dropping into the water to continue their lives.

Breeding success seems greater when several males are maintained with a single female, although communal breeding involving a dozen or so males with several females is also productive.

Cycling: Seasonal cyclings seem necessary to induce breeding in this species. From a summer high of about 16 hours of illumination and 85 to 88°F (29–31°C) temperatures, winter reductions are recommended. We think that a normal (unenhanced) photoperiod is best maintained year round. Besides the normal winter reduction of the hours of daily illumination, the relative humidity, actual humidity, and temperature need to be lowered. We recommend that this winter regimen last no less than 60 days (90 to 120 days would be better). During this period, daytime highs in the low 70s F (21–23°C) and nighttime lows in the low 60s F (16–18°C) are recommended. With slowed metabolisms, the frogs will require less food than usual during their weeks of cooling. We suggest further that the size of the individual feed insects be reduced somewhat.

For the summertime cycling, a subsequent increase in temperature, relative humidity, and misting frequency will induce greater activity, ovulation, and spermatogenesis within a week or two.

If their home terrarium is set up properly, the treefrogs may be bred there. If adequate water is not available, you'll need to move the breeding groups to a special breeding tank. These tanks usually contain 2 or 3 inches (5–7.6 cm) of water, a misting mechanism, plants or other supports for the egg clusters, temperature control, and a means of providing food to the adults.

Calls: The breeding vocalizations are coarse, single-syllable notes, which do not differ greatly (if at all) from territoriality calls. The notes are regularly, but not rapidly, repeated. Receptive females are drawn to the calls of the males. The males often cease calling and approach the females once the latter are seen. Amplexus is axillary (the male grasps the female immediately behind the forearms).

Clutches: Hatches contain from 20 to 75 eggs and are typically glued to the leaves of plants that overhang the water. Captive females often choose a spot several inches above the water on the aquarium glass as a deposition site. This location has proved precarious, since condensation on the glass often dislodges the eggs, and they fall into the water and die. It is better to gently remove the eggs from the glass and place them on a leaf (or other support) a few inches above the water. Keep in mind that the tiny new tadpoles will need to be able to either drop directly into the water or reach the water with a few flips of their body after hatching. Tadpoles denied access to the water after hatching will die.

Often as many as three or four clutches of eggs are deposited in a single night by a female. She carries the quiescent male on her back from site to site and may sit for lengthy periods in the water between depositions to replenish the fluid in her bladder. Adequate water is necessary to ensure the proper consistency of the jellylike outer egg casing. The glutinous "jelly" is clear; the eggs themselves are greenish.

Tadpoles: The time required for the development of the eggs and the growth and metamorphosis of the tadpoles is largely dependent on temperature (78–85°F or 25–29°C seems ideal). Hatching can occur in as few as five or as many as 11 days. The tadpole stage can last from 40 to 60 days.

The newly metamorphosed treefroglets have round (rather than vertically elliptical) pupils and yellow irides (irises). It may take nearly three weeks for the elliptical pupils and red irides to develop.

Within a few days of becoming froglets, the metamorphs will have developed an almost insatiable appetite. Because of their rapid growth rate they are especially prone to MBD (metabolic bone disease) at this stage of life. Feed them heavily and frequently, and dust all food items with a good-quality vitamin D_3 and calcium mixture.

Have a ready and steady supply of tiny feed insects available before you breed these (or any other) frogs. The newly metamorphosed babies are virtual "eating machines."

White's Treefrog

My introduction to White's treefrog, now called *Litoria caerulea*, occurred in the 1950s. A small shipment of reptiles and amphibians from Australia included a few containers marked "White's Treefrogs." They arrived unsolicited and were therefore a surprise.

The raised supratympanal ridges impart a comical expression to the White's treefrog, Litoria caerulea.

When I opened the cups I found a series of hefty little jade-green frogs. They sat quietly, with bulging eyes, perhaps wondering what was going on. Set up in terrariums, these little frogs grew, and grew some more. They survived for years.

Shortly after the arrival of those frogs, Australia closed its borders to the exportation of wildlife. More than two decades passed before I again saw representatives of the species.

Now, as a result of innumerable captive breeding programs, these frogs—which only a few years ago were considered rare—are readily available in nearly every pet shop in the United States and Europe, usually at prices below $25.

Australia is their main geographic range, but White's treefrogs are also found on many of the islands of the Torres Strait and in New Guinea.

Appearance: For a treefrog, the White's is large. Some females (the larger of the sexes) attain an SVL of 4.5 inches (11.4 cm), although most specimens are an inch (2.5 cm) or so smaller. With a natural tendency toward heaviness (and a captive tendency toward real obesity), White's treefrogs attain impressive size. Their bulk, green coloration, and propensity toward corpulence have resulted in a variety of common names, including Australian green, giant green, and dumpy treefrog. The females of this species tend to develop heavy supratympanal folds that jut out over the eyes. In some particularly old and obese specimens these ridges become so enlarged and pendulous that they droop over the eyes, partially obscuring vision.

White's treefrogs are also long-lived. Many records of 20-year life-spans exist, and it is probable that more than 25 years could be attained.

Color: The "normal" coloration of the White's treefrog is jade green, although its specific scientific name, *caerulea,* means "dark blue." The name may have been gained in one of two ways. First, preserved specimens—those used for scientific description—turn blue. Second, some living *caerulea* are blue: A few display attractive shades of blue green or, more rarely, true blue.

The blue coloration can be natural or created. *Caerulea* kept in darkened terrariums have a tendency to turn blue, as do those fed a diet of insects deficient in beta-carotene (the inadequate diet may induce anemia). Occasional true-blue mutations can occur among clutches of otherwise normally colored metamorphs. Some specimens have a variable amount of white spotting on their dorsum. Herpetoculturists are now line-breeding specimens in an attempt to increase the amount of white.

Diet: White's treefrogs consume a wide variety of live foods. It matters little to the frogs whether they eat crickets, giant mealworms, harmless lepidopteran caterpillars, pinky mice, or smaller frogs. In fact, White's treefrogs will consume significantly smaller specimens of their own species, as well as other frog species, with as much gusto as they display when enjoying a vitamin-dusted cricket. Choose cagemates carefully.

Remember to dust the foods with a good vitamin D_3 and calcium powder before feeding your treefrogs. Metabolic bone disease can most definitely occur in White's (and other) treefrogs. Calcium is needed more regularly by fast-growing White's treefroglets and probably by ovulating female adults. Commercially raised crickets are notably deficient in calcium. And remember that while one calcium dusting per week may be sufficient for an adult frog, two or even three weekly applications are better for fast-growing babies.

Caging: When enough attention is given to their husbandry, White's treefrogs are among the most easily kept amphibians. Their quiet demeanor, readiness to eat, and (when adult) somewhat comical appearance endear them to many people who otherwise dislike herptiles.

Though still most of the time, White's treefrogs can be quite ambulatory. They walk in hand-over-hand fashion along their arboreal highways, and if startled (this species is so laid-back that startling it might take concerted effort on your part) they display unexpectedly prodigious leaps.

A few new metamorphs—those no longer than 1 inch (2.5 cm) from snout to vent—can be kept in a 5 or 10 gallon (20 or 38 L) tank, but adults require much larger tanks. A 20-gallon (75 L) "high" terrarium may suffice for a particularly inactive specimen, but normally active individuals will do much better in a terrarium that holds between 29 and 50 (110–200 L) gallons. In suitable weather, White's treefrogs thrive in outdoor cages of wood and wire (containing plants and a water dish) and are particularly at home in heavily planted greenhouses.

Their desiccation-resistant, glandular skin allows these treefrogs to inhabit areas of relatively sparse rainfall. Keep in mind the fact that constant moisture is neither necessary nor desirable for frogs of this sort. Allow some drying between sprinklings. Provide numerous horizontal, above-ground perches. Their diameter should be equal to or slightly greater than that of the frogs, not because the frogs are so heavy but because they are not very agile: A wider perch is easier to grasp. Sections of giant bamboo are especially favored. The frogs will not only sit on top of lateral sections, but when wishing to hide will back themselves into the stem hollows. Although treefrogs will clamber among branches of small diameter, they prefer to rest on larger, more secure perches. These (and other treefrogs) may also rest while securely stuck to the glass of the terrarium, on the upright cage braces, or, if in a well-planted greenhouse, on the leaves or in the leaf axils of banana trees or other such large-leafed plants.

The terrarium for the White's treefrog can be as elaborate or simple as one wants. Adequate space, a source of fresh water, cleanliness, and perching areas are all this species needs. Additional cage furniture may be added at your discretion. The substrate for the terrarium may be a few sheets of newsprint, kraft paper, cypress mulch, or plain (lacking perlite or vermiculite) potting soil. The first two materials make cleaning the terrarium easier; the latter two create a more "finished" look. Plants also can be used, either in small pots sunk to their lip in the substrate, or—if hardy species—planted directly in the substrate.

Maintaining treefrogs requires escape-proof cages; maintaining White's treefrogs requires well-ventilated escape-proof cages. Whether your frogs live in a cage with a step-through door or in a terrarium with a top, your means of access needs a tight-fitting barrier that also provides adequate ventilation. Screen (or fine-mesh hardware cloth) obviously is better for a top or door than glass.

Daytime terrarium temperatures of 85°F (29°C) and nighttime lows of 68 to 75°F (20–24°C) are best, although White's treefrogs can survive temperatures considerably above and below the suggested parameters. We maintained the species outdoors in southwest Florida, where daytime summer temperatures routinely exceed 94°F (34°C) and winter nighttime lows occasionally drop to 45°F (7°C). In their cages of wood and wire, the White's treefrogs seemed to suffer adversely from neither extreme. However, it was apparent that they were more alert in the 68 to 85°F (19–29°C) range.

Cage cleanliness is especially important in preventing the spread of disease. Like all other frogs, White's treefrogs absorb most of their moisture requirements through their skin. The moist, permeable skin will also absorb any pathogens present. Pathogens can be spread and absorbed from contaminated water or through direct contact with feces. Mucus, dried skin, and excrement will be regularly smeared on terrarium glass, too. Spray the glass regularly and wash it at least once a week. Because of the absorbency of these frogs' skin, it is best to use plain water when cleaning terrarium glass. If a disinfectant is used, the entire tank must be rinsed thoroughly before the frogs are replaced. Outdoor cages are a little easier to maintain and clean. During our Florida rainy season it was necessary only to make certain that sufficient fresh water, in periodically sterilized bowls, was present. The rains would wash, rinse, and otherwise cleanse the cage. During the dry season the water dishes were tended daily and the cages were sprayed copiously with water from a hose.

Breeding: While many hobbyists may keep a White's treefrog merely to enjoy an exotic pet, an ever-growing number of reptile and amphibian enthusiasts are choosing to breed their specimens. White's are among the amphibian species that can be bred with only a little preparation.

As with many amphibians and reptiles, a period of cooling at the time of year when day lengths are shortest will be an important part of the reproductive cycling procedure for your White's. Those we kept outdoors in Florida cycled naturally; indoors the cycling must be done manually. The chapter on breeding anurans (see page 34) will give you specifics, but the basics can be reviewed here easily.

To breed your treefrogs it will, of course, be necessary to have both sexes present. Visual determination of the sex of subadult specimens is impossible; visual determination of the sex of adult specimens is difficult. Adult male White's treefrogs often develop a darker throat with looser skin than that of the female. The loose skin accommodates the swelling of the vocal sac during chorusing. Males are also slightly smaller than the females, and when sitting quietly they may keep their forelimbs slightly less flexed than the females. If properly cycled, prior to breeding male White's treefrogs will also develop darkened, roughened nuptial (grasping) pads on the outsides of their thumbs. These pads enable the male to retain his grasp on the female during amplexus (the breeding embrace).

Properly cycled males will initially respond by producing oft-repeated, lengthy series of low-pitched croaks. These songs of ardor will further stimulate the ovulating females. Amplexus should then follow.

Eggs and tadpoles: After egg deposition, keep the eggs at 78 to 88°F (26–30°C). Hatching should begin within two days. The newly hatched tadpoles may appear inert—even dead—but will begin to show limited activity within two days of hatching. Three or four days later, their reserves of egg yolk fully utilized and mouthparts more solidified, the tadpoles will begin searching for food. Trout chow, catfish chow, tropical fish "fry" food, hard-boiled egg yolk (perhaps the messiest of the foods suggested), and other such sources of animal protein will be consumed in ever-increasing amounts.

At suitable temperatures, with good water conditions, ample feedings, and no crowding, the growth rates of the

Although less placid than the related White's treefrog, the white-lipped treefrog, Litoria infrafrenata, *is steadily gaining in popularity.*

tadpoles will be rapid. If conditions are optimum, metamorphosis may occur in just over four weeks, but it can take up to two months and, rarely, a little longer. Once the forelimbs appear, metamorphosis is usually complete within a week.

Froglets: As they prepare for their emergence from the water, the jaw-parts of the tadpoles change from rasping, scraping mechanisms to the wide, smilingly predacious countenances of the metamorphed froglets. Dietary considerations change. The metamorphs will, from that point on, require vast quantities of suitably sized, vitamin-enhanced insects or other arthropods. Termites, small crickets, sow bugs, flies, and the like will be eagerly accepted.

The White-lipped Treefrog

In recent years, a large congeneric of the White's treefrog has become available: the white-lipped treefrog (*Litoria infrafrenata*), indigenous to the York Peninsula of northern Queensland, New Guinea, and many nearby islands and island groups. Overall, the species seems more tolerant of—even dependent on—a higher relative humidity than the White's treefrog, but it is much less cold-tolerant. The white-lipped treefrog is also considerably more nervous in demeanor than the White's, reacting to excessive handling by exuding white, apparently noxious, skin secretions.

Appearance: Like White's treefrogs, white-lipped treefrogs are variably colored. Individual frogs are capable of chameleonlike changes from olive brown to bright leaf green. Interpopulation differences also exist. The color of an individual specimen may be directly related to surrounding environmental conditions. "Happy," healthy white-lipped treefrogs maintained in warm, spacious, sunlit or otherwise amply illuminated conditions tend to be a much more attractive, brighter green than specimens kept in cool, dark, crowded surroundings.

81

A native of Cuba and other West Indian islands, the Cuban treefrog, Osteopilus septentrionalis, *has been established in south Florida for several decades. Adult females can exceed 5 inches (12.7 cm) in length.*

The skin of the white-lipped treefrog has a granular appearance, usually most noticeable on the sides. Supratympanal ridges are well, but not overly, developed.

Males may be slightly smaller than females, but size does not seem to be a definitive criterion in sexing. Males also have a very slightly darker throat than females, and the throat skin, which males swell into a vocal sac when chorusing, is less taut. The darkened, roughened excrescences known as nuptial pads (present on the outer sides of the thumbs of males) become noticeable when males are in breeding readiness.

Caging: This species has less tolerance for cold, but otherwise its captive needs are similar to those of the White's treefrog.

Breeding: This species has not been bred so frequently as White's treefrog, perhaps because fewer are available and sexing is difficult. It seems that temperatures in the low 70s F (21–23°C), in combination with a reduced photoperiod for six to eight weeks, will cycle these beautiful treefrogs for breeding.

Other Treefrogs

Cuban Treefrog, *Osteopilus septentrionalis*

This species, introduced into Florida several decades ago, attains a size larger than any of our native treefrogs. Cuban treefrogs, voracious predators, consume virtually any insect, other amphibian, lizard, tiny snake, nestling bird, or mouse they encounter. Where Cuban treefrogs are common in their range on Florida's various Keys and southern peninsula, there is often a marked decrease in the populations of smaller native treefrogs.

Appearance: Although somewhat variable in color, Cuban treefrogs are usually some shade of tan, olive, or gray. Some specimens may have darker dorsal marblings, while a rare specimen may even be uniformly turquoise in dorsal coloration. Most are rather dull.

Cuban treefrogs have particularly noxious skin secretions. Should you accidentally rub your eyes or put your fingers in your mouth prior to washing, you will regret your oversight.

The 2- to 2.5-inch (5.1–6.3 cm) male Cuban treefrogs are much smaller than their mates. It seems quite probable that the males often survive only a year or two in the wild. Females, on the other hand, often live for more than five years, and some are known to last a decade in the wild. Captive females have lived for more than 15 years. Occasional females exceed 5 inches (12.7 cm) in SVL (snout-to-vent length). Impressive frogs with huge toepads, they sit quietly in ambush, engulfing whatever prey has the misfortune of passing them by.

Caging: The Cuban treefrogs offered by pet shops and specialty dealers are usually in the 2- to 3-inch (5–7.6 cm) range. Wild-collected, most will live for years if cared for properly. As their common name suggests, Cuban treefrogs are natives of Cuba and the surrounding islands. Not at all cold-tolerant, they are seriously debilitated by temperatures that linger in the low 50s F (10–12°C) and killed by temperatures that fall to the low 40s F (4–6°C) and remain there for more than a few hours.

Breeding: Should you choose to try your luck at cycling Cuban treefrogs for breeding, winter lows in the 60s F (16–18°C), and a shorter photoperiod will suffice. After several weeks of cooling and long nights, placing these frogs in a warm (80–85°F or 27–29°C) rain chamber for a few days should stimulate breeding activity. The vocalizations of male Cuban treefrogs are varied, but all are variations of curious clucks, squeaks, and growls. The calls

of those that bred in our water lily tubs in Florida always reminded us of the sound made by fingers being drawn over a fully inflated wet balloon.

In its ability to change from browns and tans to light and dark greens, the barking treefrog, Hyla gratiosa is chameleon-like. The barking treefrog is a species of the southeastern coastal plain of the USA.

Although the dark-edged, enamel white stripe seen on this green treefrog, Hyla cinerea, is typical, some specimens lack the stripes entirely.

83

Often gray, both the northern and southern gray treefrogs, Hyla versicolor *and* H. chrysoscelis, *also assume a green coloration. These two frog species are extremely difficult to differentiate.*

Barking Treefrog, *Hyla gratiosa,* and Green Treefrog, *Hyla cinerea*

Two of the world's prettiest treefrog species are found in the southeastern United States. One, the green treefrog, is a slender, smooth-skinned species that derives its common name from the dorsal color in which it is typically clad. (Cold, dry, or "unhappy" specimens may assume an olive-brown to brown coloration.) Most specimens have a broad, enamel-white lateral line extending from beneath the eye to the groin. The line may be shorter or even absent in some specimens. Green treefrogs may attain a length of nearly 2.5 inches (6.4 cm). The breeding calls of this species are frequently repeated nasal honks. These have often been referred to as having a "cowbell-like quality," a simile that has eluded me altogether.

The barking treefrog is the largest species of treefrog native to the Southeast. Not only do some specimens approach (or even attain) the 2¾ inch (7 cm) mark, but they are of proportionately robust build as well. In color and pattern, this species is one

of the most variable. Within minutes an individual can change its dorsal coloration from bright green to tan, gray-green, or deep brown. In any of these colors, ocelli may be prominent or obscure, many or few, or replaced by small whitish spots. The calls of breeding males sound much like the barking of dogs. This analogy is more apt if the male is singing away from the water. If he is afloat while chorusing, his calls have a rather hollow, ringing sound.

Both the green and barking treefrogs are common and easily kept. Little effort is expended by hobbyists on attempts to breed either of these species, perhaps because wild-collected specimens remain so readily available in pet shops. Refer to the chapter on reproductive techniques (page 34) and the section on gray treefrogs (below) for suggestions on breeding.

Gray Treefrogs, *Hyla versicolor* complex

Establishing the field identity of the two gray treefrogs of the United States is well-nigh impossible. So similar are these two wide-ranging species that only chromosomal analysis can differentiate the females with certainty. The males may be differentiated by their vocalizations, if the calls are made and compared at the same temperature. The relatively slow trill (pulse rate) of the more northerly of these two sibling species, *Hyla versicolor,* produces a beautiful, musical fluting. At the same temperature, the much faster pulse rate of the more southerly *H. chrysoscelis* produces a rather harsh staccato. For our purposes it is sufficient to group both as "gray treefrogs."

Although gray treefrogs vary from chalk white to lime green in color, if they are left to rest quietly at agreeable temperatures their dorsal (back) color will eventually return to some shade of gray. An irregular, darker figure (rather like a vaguely star-shaped piece of lichen) adorns the back of both species, and both have a light spot reaching from the edge of the upper lip to the eye. The dorsal skin of the 2¼-inch (5.7 cm) gray treefrogs is roughened, but not nearly so warty as that of a toad. The concealed surfaces of the hind limbs and the groin are black-reticulated golden orange to rich orange.

The two species may be found across most of the eastern half of our continent, from extreme southern Canada to the Gulf Coast. Gray treefrogs are persistently arboreal and seldom seen in terrestrial or aquatic situations, except during the breeding season. Even then, males often call while sitting in pondside trees and shrubs.

Bird-voiced treefrog *H. avivoca*:

In the deep tupelo and magnolia swamps of the Southeast dwells a somewhat smaller treefrog that is much the same as the grays in dorsal color, but with dorsal skin a little smoother. This is the bird-voiced treefrog, a species quite easily distinguished by its wonderful lilting, tremulous call. Unlike the gray treefrogs, both of which have orange coloring beneath the rear limbs, the groin color of the bird-voiced treefrog is pale green to pale yellowish white. This species is even more steadfastly arboreal than the grays, but it may occasionally be found crossing rainswept roadways during spring and summer thunderstorms.

Canyon treefrog *H. arenicolor*:

This species resembles the gray treefrogs but has sandier body tones. The darker, lichenate dorsal marking is represented by a series of small blotches rather than a single large one,

and the light marking below the eye is bordered by dark bars. This western treefrog occurs in Texas' Big Bend region, western New Mexico, most of Arizona, and southern Utah, and ranges far southward into Mexico. Canyon treefrogs, more terrestrial than the other treefrogs discussed here, often are encountered among boulders, escarpments, and similar formations. The voice of this robust species is a harsh, low-pitched staccato.

Breeding: Although the treefrogs of the United States are easily maintained on diets of vitamin-enhanced insects and live long lives as captives, little effort has been made by hobbyists to breed them. A few hobbyists have bred the gray and bird-voiced treefrogs in rather large greenhouses by allowing considerable winter cooling and a natural photoperiod. For breeding indoors, it would be necessary to cycle the frogs through the seasons artificially. Cool temperatures and a reduced photoperiod during the winter months are among the most important aspects of any cycling attempt. See page 35.

Although not colorful, the canyon treefrog, Hyla arenicolor, of the western United States and adjacent Mexico is locally abundant and very hardy.

Typical Frogs: Family Ranidae

The American Bullfrog

The family Ranidae is represented on all continents of the world save Antarctica. Perhaps its most familiar member is the bullfrog. Heard in many wilderness movies, the "jug-o-rum" calls of the American bullfrog, *Rana catesbeiana*, are nearly as well known to moviegoers across the world as to Americans visiting rural picnic sites. The booming voices of the males echo across lakes, marshes, and slowly flowing rivers and vie with the sputters of outboard motors for supremacy.

Appearance: Everything about this magnificent frog is big—its size, its spawn, its tadpoles, its appetite, its voice, its leaping ability. Adult female bullfrogs, slightly the larger sex, have been known to attain a snout-to-vent length (SVL) of 8 inches (20.4 cm). Females may lay 12,000 eggs annually, and the tadpoles can measure nearly 7 inches (17.7 cm) long at two years of age, immediately before metamorphosis.

Diet: Bullfrogs are predacious. They have been known to eat baby muskrats, other frogs, snakes, turtles, and salamanders, and even to catch low-flying birds on the wing.

Depending upon their size, captive bullfrogs will eat crickets, worms, and mice. A commercial food is now on the market.

Caging: The only bad aspect of keeping a bullfrog in captivity is its jumping ability. Initially a nervous captive may repeatedly jump into the sides of its container when startled (and at first, it may be startled by everything). This tendency has rather discouraged hobbyists, and the creature is not often seen in collections. That is unfortunate, for in this day of diminishing amphibian populations, the bullfrog seems to be one species whose numbers continue to swell.

Originally a species of eastern North America, the American bullfrog has been introduced into areas far west and south of its natural range. Bullfrog farming (to supply frogs' legs for culinary use) was once a fairly large business. Most frog farms are now defunct, but in most areas into which they were introduced the bullfrogs have thrived and expanded in range. The presence of the immense, voracious bullfrog in our Pacific state lakes, rivers, and farm ponds, in combination with such problems as drought, acidification, and ozone-level changes, has wreaked havoc among the populations of the smaller native frog species. Where large populations of red and yellow-legged frogs (*R. aurora* ssp. and *R. muscosa*) once were encountered, now only the introduced bullfrog is still seen with regularity.

A bullfrog will thrive as a captive if you move rather slowly around its enclosure. A pair we kept lived for many years in a strongly filtered 50-gallon (200 L) aquarium. The tank was a little more than half full, and was decorated with floating plants and a thick stub of limb that protruded from the water at an angle. The female bullfrog often used the limb as a haulout area, but the male was almost always to be seen floating complacently amid the vegetation. Both frogs were "tame" enough to accept mice, minnows, and strips of lean meat from my fingers. Once in a great while the male would indulge in a series of "jug-o-rums" that would set the water to vibrating as the calls echoed through the house.

Pyxies

Appearance and behavior: The South African pyxie or African bullfrog, *Pyxicephalus adspersus*, is much less nervous than its American counterpart. But don't let the diminutive name "pyxie" fool you. These are not petite toadlets. At nearly 10 inches (25.4 cm) in SVL (females attain only half that size), the males of this hefty anuran species attain an even greater bulk than the females of our American bullfrog. Pyxies differ radically from bullfrogs in new-captive behavior. The adult pyxie is quiet, almost "laid-back" in demeanor. A rather poor jumper, the pyxie is not at all disposed to smash into the glass sides of its terrarium if startled.

The African pyxie differs from our bullfrog in other ways, too. While our bullfrog is primarily aquatic and restricted to permanent bodies of water, the pyxie is largely terrestrial, reportedly spending more than half the year "burrowed in" in dry habitats. It is induced to activity by seasonal rains and breeds in temporary waterholes. The pyxie lays fewer than half the number of eggs produced by our bullfrog, but 5,000 eggs a year is inarguably a goodly number.

Pyxies are very popular among herptile enthusiasts, being edged out of first place by the ornate horned frog. Like the ornates, pyxies have earned respect by refusing to be cowed. They have three well-

America's largest frog is the bullfrog, Rana catesbeiana. *Originally an eastern species, it is now firmly established all the way to the Pacific coast.*

developed odontoid structures at the front of the lower jaw—and if hard pressed they are not reluctant to bite.

Diet: Pyxies consume any prey that they can overcome and swallow. Adult captive males have been known to tackle good-sized rats, and an adult mouse is hardly more than a very small bite. Captives adapt easily to feeding upon rats, mice, and chicks. Pyxies are quite cannibalistic and will not hesitate to eat frogs of their own or other species. This tendency is evident even in new metamorphs, which will prey on siblings if hungry.

Caging: Because of their rather sedentary nature, captive pyxies do not require large terrariums. A 20-gallon (75 L) long tank is usually sufficient for a single adult male. Pyxies can be kept either in about 1 inch (2.5 cm) of water or in a terrestrial setup, whichever your prefer. If you opt for the former, remember to check the water cleanliness once, or even twice daily. A frog this large can thoroughly foul its water in a matter of minutes. Filtration may not keep the water

Juvenile African bullfrogs, Pyxicephalus adspersus, *have prominent light vertebral lines. These obscure with growth.*

clean enough; you may be faced with frequent water changes, using dechlorinated water.

Breeding: Pyxies are readily bred in captivity. They require the usual cycling, and you can induce reproductive readiness by misting for several evenings. The alternative method is hormonal inducement of ovulation and spermatogenesis. Breeders often utilize children's wading pools as breed-

ing containers for these large frogs. In warmer climates, natural atmospheric phenomena may stimulate pyxies to breed. Be prepared to make frequent and extensive water changes and to offer ample food to the tadpoles if you hope to be successful with this immense species.

Dwarf pyxies: A much smaller species of pyxie is occasionally offered for sale. This is *P. delalandei*, to which the common name of dwarf pyxie is often applied. As far as we know, it is not being bred in captivity.

Other Typical Ranids

Pig Frogs

Although it may be distressing for reptile and amphibian enthusiasts to realize this, Ranidae are more widely known for the food value of their legs than for their appeal as curious, interesting pets. Frog gigging remains an income-producing "sport" in many areas of the world, and it is nowhere more avidly pursued than in the swamps and marshes of the southeastern United States. There, equipped with sharpened tridents and headlamps, frog hunters ply the

Despite a sedentary lifestyle, the tadpole of the pig frog is of streamlined appearance.

Big, belligerent and hardy, adult African bullfrogs, Pyxicephalus adspersus, *are truly impressive beasts.*

The overall shape of this green frog tadpole indicates a species generalized in both habits and habitats.

glades and flooded grasslands in Johnboats and airboats in search of pig frogs, *R. grylio*. This species derives its common name from the porcine notes of the males.

The toll taken by these hunters is immense. Since few ranid frogs are popular "pet" species, the pet trade is of little consequence to ranid populations.

Smaller Species

Cascade frog: Besides the bullfrog and pyxie, smaller and odder ranid species are occasionally available. One such is the Southeast Asian cascade frog, *Rana livida*, a beautiful brown-sided species with a forest-green back. It has well-developed toe pads that undoubtedly assist its movement in rocky mountain torrents. If kept cool and supplied with sufficient insects, this alert, 2-inch-long (5 cm) species will do quite well in a semi-aquatic terrarium.

American leopard frogs, *Rana pipiens* complex, are often offered for sale by both pet dealers and biological supply houses. The frogs, so named for the squarish blotches adorning their dorsa, are familiar to biology students because they are commonly used for dissection. In the wild, many species of leopard frogs are increasingly rare, their snoring chuckles heard ever less frequently. That is the case with the northern leopard frog, *R. pipiens*. However, populations of the southern species, *R. (utricularia) sphenocehala*, seem to be holding their own or actually increasing. The cause of the population decreases is not entirely clear. It is currently thought to be the result of several phenomena, including habitat degradation, acidification of the waters in which the frogs breed, increases in ultraviolet radiation due to ozone depletion, and pressure by collectors for the pet and biological supply industries. Dr. Fredric L. Frye has informed us that one of the major causes for the

The Asian cascade frog, Rana livida, *prefers cool, rock-strewn streams and brooks. It is an agile, streamlined frog that is only occasionally available to hobbyists.*

decline of *R. pipiens* is the herpes virus luckei adenocarcinoma, which attacks their kidneys. Most northern leopard frogs now carry this virus. Many states are now protecting their populations of leopard frogs and striving to reverse the habitat degradation. Even snake collectors may unwittingly put pressure on leopard frog populations, since it is the members of this species complex that are most frequently sold as food

Although populations of the northern leopard frog, Rana pipiens, *are diminishing, those of the southern species,* Rana (utricularia) sphenocephala *are holding steady or actually increasing.*

for the many specialized snakes. Among those that prefer frog-fare are water, garter, and ribbon snakes and related species.

Wood frog: Another species seen on price lists is small and subtly colored, yet one of the most beautiful of all ranid frogs. This is the little wood frog, *R. sylvatica*, indigenous to temperate North America. This woodland species seeks standing water annually for a few days of breeding. During the early spring, the chickenlike clucking notes of "woodies" can be heard from many vernal ponds. After breeding, wood frogs disperse widely into the cool, damp woodlands. Because they are both secretive and clad in earthen tones, their true population densities are unknown. Often turning as they leap, frightened wood frogs bound away from perceived danger in a series of confusingly irregular hops. This beautiful little frog with the dark "robber's mask" can be easily maintained in a woodland terrarium. Woodies have not yet been captive-bred.

Because of its mask, the American wood frog, Rana sylvatica, *is easily differentiated from other American frogs.*

Ranid Protection

Only rarely will you see a European frog or toad for sale. Because of dramatic population reductions, collection of many of the European frogs for either pet or food purposes is now prohibited. No matter what the country, of course, the ban on collection does not provide total protection. In many areas of the industrialized world, automobiles continue to take a terrible toll on road-crossing frogs, especially on rainy spring evenings when breeding aggregations of frogs, toads, and treefrogs are queuing up in ponds. But the installation of crossing culverts, flanked on each end by low fences, channels the aggregating amphibians to and from their breeding ponds in safety.

Our tip: Most ranid frogs will do quite well as terrarium animals and many are readily available in the wild. Be sure to check applicable game laws before collecting any. Many species are now fully protected at the state level and some at the federal and international levels.

Madagascar's Magnificent Mantellas

Until a very few years ago, the brightly colored mantellas, Madagascar's equivalents of the arrow-poison frogs, were virtually unknown to all but scientists. Even today new species continue to be described and forms long known to science redescribed. Mantellas arriving in this country are often imported under such designations as *M. mysteriosa*, a contrived name that clearly indicates the necessity of continued study. The truth is that many, if not most, of these magnificent miniatures remain mysterious to American hobbyists (and scientists).

Why do these little frogs remain cloaked in such confusion? Perhaps it is because the few forests that remain on Madagascar are only now being explored, and it is these habitats that are the strongholds of mantella speciation. Thus many populations of mantellas are being encountered for the first time by scientists and collectors alike.

The continued arrival of "new-form" mantellas once again illustrates the limited scope of our knowledge of the herpetofauna of Madagascar. The island is in dire need of exploration and viable conservation practices, neither of which, because of the country's relative inaccessibility and need for currency, is an easily attainable goal. Sadly, as the forests are explored they are often targeted for logging, a practice that reduces correspondingly the habitats of forest-dependent creatures—the mantellas among them. Even as we are beginning to know and understand them, the populations of mantellas are dwindling.

The mantellas are sufficiently distinct to form their own subfamily, the Mantellinae.

For the most part, these frogs are natives of the forests of Madagascar. The painted mantella, *M. madagascariensis*, occurs also on the islands of Betsileo and Réunion. Mantellas are said to be weak swimmers, shunning deep water. That is not necessarily true; it may be that these species are unable to swim for protracted periods. At least three of the species/morphs we have maintained enter water readily and, despite their lack of webs, are able to swim. While in the water the toes of each rear foot are closed together, rather than widely spread.

While mantellas seem to prefer the environs of shallow pools or intermittent streams, they may also utilize ephemeral pools formed during Madagascar's rainy season. One or more of the mantella species may become almost dormant during the dry season, being triggered to activity, including breeding, by the first substantial rains.

The tiny golden mantella, Mantella aurantiaca *of Madagascar, is one of the most beautiful frogs in the world. In habits and habitats the Madagascar mantellas parallel the neotropical arrow-poison frogs.*

Species Accounts

Since several *Mantella* species and certain morphs of others have no accepted common name, we will attempt to assign appropriate ones for the purpose of this book. We need to add that the taxonomy of the entire genus is changing. While it seems certain that a great many more species exist than are now currently described, and that some of the names now in use may be synonymized with others, widespread acceptance of proposed changes is slow in coming. American researchers are reluctant to accept many of the hypotheses of their European colleagues, and vice versa. With that in mind, we have incorporated few of the proposed name changes here. Rather, we have used the nomenclature, be it accurate or inaccurate, under which these species are most often marketed in the American pet trade.

Mantella aurantiaca has three separate color morphs. Perhaps the best known of all of the mantellas is the little golden mantella, the golden phase of *M. aurantiaca*. It is found in the isolated patches of rain-forest habitat that

Currently this magnificent miniature is classified as a color phase of Mantella aurantiaca, *but the ruby mantella may eventually prove to be a new species.*

remain in southeastern Madagascar. The golden mantella is an intense rich golden hue that is sometimes overlaid with a blush of red. Reported to be a lowland form, this frog is capable of withstanding more warmth than highland species.

The brightly colored Mantella madagascariensis *has long been a herpetocultural favorite. It is commonly called the "painted mantella."*

Two other morphs of this species appear less frequently on dealer lists. The first, often called the ruby mantella, occurs in colors that range from an intense tomato red to vermilion. It is shipped as an "aridland form" of *aurantiaca.* The other morph has been imported since 1993 or 1994. It is similar in color to the ruby phase, but in addition has a black spot on the tympanum (external eardrum). Both red morphs seem slightly smaller than the golden mantella.

Mantella madagascariensis, the mountain-dwelling painted mantella, was long thought to be a variant of another species, *M. cowani* (see page 94). The painted mantella of eastern Madagascar is unquestionably the most variably colored of the mantellas. If all the frogs imported as this species truly are this species, the term "variable" might be more apt.

The painted mantella has a black dorsum and groin, yellow to lime green or blue sides and forelimbs, and orange hind limbs that are reticulated with black. Some may have either a brown head or a brown head and brown rear limbs. The thighs may be vermilion. To add to the confusion, where the ranges of the painted and the golden mantellas overlap, hybridizing is known. This adds more variability to the coloration, and confusion to the taxonomy.

M. laevigata: Despite its bright colors, the painted mantella is by no means the prettiest member of the genus. It was not until 1994 that we had an opportunity to meet *M. laevigata.* The pictures we had seen had not done justice to this beautifully colored, slightly elongate frog with big toepads. *Laevigata* is black except for the dorsum, which is lime-green. *M. laevigata* is more persistently arboreal than the other members of the genus, and only recently did we learn that this species breeds in water-filled holes in

The true identification of Mantella myste-riosa, *the "mystery mantella" is currently under investigation.*

As currently described, Mantella crocea *occurs in two distinct color phases, a bronze and a green. This is another species that requires additional research.*

standing trees. Since there are other black and green mantellas, "arboreal mantella" might be an appropriate common name for this small species.

Mantella viridis: Its common name, green mantella, seems fitting for this white-lipped, black-masked green species. The hind limbs may fade to cobalt and the lower sides may display a bluish overcast. One of the larger mantellas, *viridis* attains a robust 1⅜ inches (3.4 cm) in length.

M. crocea: If the identification provided is correct, the saffron mantella is imported in at least four color phases. One phase has a base color of pale yellowish green, another of russet, a third is mostly yellow, and a fourth is variably black-peppered red. The first two phases have black masks and black anterior sides of variable extent. The green phase usually has orange rear limbs, and both the green and the russet phases often have vermilion on the concealed surfaces of the thighs. (You may see the latter two morphs referred to as *Mantella myste-riosa* on dealer's lists.) The specific name *crocea* refers to saffron coloration, but seemingly comparatively few are so colored. Yet, "saffron mantella" may be as good a common name as any for this variable species.

M. expectata: Sporting a green dorsum, black lateral surfaces, and cobalt lip and limbs, this frog is rather newly

The green mantella, M. viridis, is one of the larger and hardier species.

The black-sided Mantella betsileo *is not imported as frequently as some of its more brightly colored relatives.*

described. The degree of color variability and the frog's habits remain unknown.

M. betsileo: Of the mantellas most frequently seen, brown mantella is the least colorful. This central Madagascan frog has a copper to brown dorsum and black sides and venter.

Mantella cowani *is not yet a species commonly seen in herpetoculture. This frog, clad in the colors of Halloween, is certainly one of the most beautiful members of the genus.*

M. cowani: In March, 1994, we finally had an opportunity to not only meet, but acquire a few specimens of the very beautiful orange-banded mantella. This creature, strikingly clad in bands of brilliant orange against a ground color of jet black, vies in color intensity and hue with the brightest of the New World's arrow-poison frogs. Since there is no common name for these creatures, we'll call them "orange-banded mantellas," because of the brilliant bands of fire-orange that cross the rear limbs. Additionally, the frogs have a fire-orange spot at the apex of each forelimb, a tiny orange crescent anterior to the eye, and several jade green spots on the venter. All frogs of this form arrived in robust condition and were very active and alert. All fed immediately on termites, sugar ants, and pinhead crickets.

Quite unlike many other mantellas, which often shun water unless hard pressed and then seem ill-at-ease until again on land, orange-banded mantellas leap into the water and submerge when startled. They swim with their toes closed tightly together. Indeed, for a species with webless toes they seem remarkably at home in the aquatic element.

Considerations for All Mantellas

Appearance: These are small, beautiful frogs. Their snout-to-vent length ranges from ¾ to 1¼ inches (1.9–3.2 cm).

Sexing: Sexual dimorphism is slight in mantellas, and visual differentiation relies largely on a series of comparisons among several frogs of the same species. The males are usually not quite so robust and are slightly smaller than the females. Males often sit in a more upright position with their forelimbs straightened. Only the males vocalize, but the sounds are soft and may be difficult to hear, even in a terrarium. The calls of some species have been likened to "tinking" notes, and those of others to splattering droplets of water. The calls of still other species have yet to be described.

Color and toxicity: The members of the genus *Mantella* are every bit as brilliant in coloration as the much-lauded arrow-poison frogs of Latin America, and their rain forest habitats even more imperiled. Although the colors of the mantellas may serve a warning function, little is known about the actual toxicity of the skin secretions.

Diet: Mantellas are tiny, and their food must be tinier. Crickets of all sizes are commercially available. It will probably be necessary to order by mail the tiny sizes you will need for your mantellas. Those sold as "pinhead size" are a good staple. The smallest mantellas seem to enjoy these tiny crickets, but as the frogs mature and grow larger, they feed less and less avidly upon crickets. Fruit flies, termites, and other such insects seem to be more eagerly accepted. One of the best methods of procuring food, weather conditions permitting, is to sweep an insect net through the tall grasses of a vacant field. A variety of minuscule insects will usually be found in your net.

If wild insects are provided as food, vitamin/mineral augmentation will probably be unnecessary. If crickets and fruit flies are the main diet, they should be dusted occasionally with a good, finely powdered vitamin D_3, and mineral supplement. We prefer to provide our frogs with numerous smaller, as opposed to a few larger, food insects.

Caging: When properly kept, mantellas are hardy captives. The basics are the same, whether you are keeping a couple because you think them pretty and interesting or hope to breed them. The major difference would be in the size of your container and the number of frogs therein. While a 5-gallon (20 L)

terrarium may be sufficient for a couple of mantellas, we provide larger quarters when possible. We believe a 10-gallon tank (38 L) to be more suitable, and we would opt for a minimum of a 20-gallon (75 L) "long" for a breeding group of these frogs. The larger the terrarium, the easier it is to maintain.

As captives, mantellas are most comfortable at a temperature range of 68°F to 76°F (19°C–24°C); remember that many of these are montane species. Mantellas become obviously discomfited when temperatures near 80°F (27°C), and lethargic when temperatures drop much below 65°F (18°C).

Besides being agile climbers, mantellas require high humidity. All terrariums must be kept humid and tightly covered. Humidity can be maintained by using a standard aquarium hood that incorporates a fluorescent light, or by affixing plastic over a screen cover. Make it a habit to mist your terrarium lightly once or twice daily to ensure that the humidity remains high. High humidity is especially important when eggs are developing.

Terrariums may be as simple or as intricate as you wish. See the chapter on housing (page 16) for the various types of terrariums. There are several considerations to keep in mind. Small areas of seclusion—"caves"—are important to a colony of mantellas. The simplest caves, and the easiest to clean, are the opaque plastic bottoms of plastic soda containers into which a small door has been cut. More difficult to clean, but sturdy and long-lasting, are the halved inner hulls of coconuts. Moss and corkbark caves are suitable alternatives. The caves should be very near the water receptacle, for it is within the caves that the frogs will breed. Immediate proximity to the water will ensure that the newly hatched tadpoles reach that all-important element.

Breeding: In the wild, the males' vocalizations draw the females to secluded terrestrial areas near pond edges. The females lay their clutches of 12 to 30 large eggs on land, adjacent to water. The eggs are immediately fertilized by the dominant male. The eggs undergo terrestrial development, and the tadpoles either wriggle their way to the nearby water or are washed into the water by rivulets during storms. The tadpoles grow and metamorphose rapidly, and some six to eight weeks later the mantella froglets emerge from the water to begin their terrestrial existence.

At least two species, *M. aurantiaca,* the golden mantella, and *M. madagas-cariensis*, the painted mantella, have been captive-bred by American hobbyists. European herpetoculturists have bred at least one other, *M. laevigata,* a beautiful green-backed species with no common name. Although mantellas have been bred when kept as pairs, success is more likely with a group of four or five males and a single female.

Many people do not think of frogs as territorial, but in asserting dominance and establishing territory, male mantellas will engage in lengthy wrestling bouts in which the weaker contestant is actually flipped upside down onto the substrate. It is, of course, the winner that breeds the female.

Tomato Frogs and Others: Family Microhylidae

The Tomato Frogs

Picture, if you will, a frog that is flame orange in color, 4 inches (10.2 cm) in length, and as robust as any toad, and you will have a fairly accurate image of the remarkably beautiful Guinet's tomato frog, *Dyscophus guineti,* of northeastern Madagascar. If you look more closely you will see either that the orange of the back is rather heavily stippled with brighter red, or that a dark (from vague to well delineated) middorsal rhomboid is present.

Though rather obscure, these markings serve to differentiate the nonendangered Guinet's tomato frog from the endangered (but no longer very common) common tomato frog, *D. antongili,* also of northeastern Madagascar.

There is a third species, a tomato frog that is not tomato-colored: the smaller, brownish *D. insularis.* Since it is restricted in distribution to the western coast of the island, we will call this, the dullest form, the western tomato frog.

Appearance: The nocturnal tomato frogs are microhylids (tiny woodland frogs). They are members of the narrow-mouthed toad group, although there is nothing whatsoever in their general external morphology to suggest such a relationship. The heads of the *Discophus* species are neither noticeably small nor narrow.

Adults of the various tomato frogs are sexually dimorphic, with the females being nearly one third larger than the males. Of the three species, the common tomato frog is the largest, occasional females exceeding 4 inches (10.2 cm) in length. Guinet's tomato frog ranks second, the females attaining 3.5 inches (8.9 cm). The less-coveted western tomato frog is the smallest, adult females barely exceeding 2 inches (5 cm) in snout-to-vent length (SVL).

Breeding: Since the exportation of these beautiful frogs may cease at any time, it is particularly important that we learn the nuances of breeding them through several generations. Thus far we have failed to do so. There is little problem in breeding the wild-collected, naturally cycled adult frogs, but beyond that we begin to stumble noticeably. Diet, temperature regimens, or a combination of these and other factors may be responsible.

At present there are many potential breeding colonies of Guinet's tomato frogs in the United States. There are even a few colonies of common tomato frogs (mostly in zoos). The few programs that have succeeded have depended on typical cycling (including the rain/hydration chamber) in combination with hormonal augmentation.

For the cycling (slight cooling, reduction of relative and actual humidity, temperature, and photoperiod) and

Males of the Guinet's tomato frog, Dyscophus guineti, *tend to be the more brilliantly colored and less strongly patterned sex.*

construction of the rain chamber, see page 26.

Despite references to tomato frogs as denizens of roadside ditches, such places probably are their habitat only during the breeding season. It is understandable that so many records refer to ditches, for it is when the frogs are in them that the males are the most vocal. The calls are termed raucous by some observers, disharmo-

The brilliantly colored common tomato frog, Dyscophus antongili, *of Madagascar is now listed as an endangered species.*

nious by others. After breeding, these interesting microhylids disperse into nearby woodlands and become quite fossorial. They apparently emerge to feed during rainy weather.

Captive care: Tomato frogs are quite hardy, readily accepting suitably sized insects. If the frogs are large enough, they can eat pinky mice. Tomato frogs are quite temperature-tolerant and can sustain periodic temperatures of 50 to 95°F (10–35°C) with no signs of discomfort.

The Malayan Painted Frog

The pet trade in the United States offers another mycrohylid, the Malayan painted frog, *Kaloula pulchra.*

Appearance: As indicated by its alternate common name, chubby frog, the 2.5-inch-long (6.2 cm) *Kaloula* is of robust build. Despite the implications of its name of painted frog, *Kaloula pulchra* is darkly clad in earthen hues. The dark dorsum is broadly edged with a well-defined but irregular fawn-colored dorsolateral band. Below the band the sides are darker.

Breeding: If a pattern of typical cycling is followed, painted frogs can be rather easily bred. The floating eggs are strongly adhesive. *Kaloula pulchra* has one of the shortest known spans of metamorphosis. Under ideal conditions tadpoles can metamorphose in about two weeks' time.

The Narrow-mouthed Toads and Sheep Frogs

The tomato frogs have three relatives—members of the nocturnal family Microhylidae—in the United States. These are the diminutive narrow-mouthed toads and the sheep frog.

Appearance: All are superficially similar in appearance, being only slightly more than 1 inch (2.5 cm) in SVL and having tiny, pointed heads. A fold of skin across the nape gives the erroneous impression that these frogs can withdraw their heads (in the manner of an anuran turtle). Apparently the skin-fold can be shrugged forward to help dislodge biting ants (ants of certain species are favored food insects) from the eye area.

When frightened or chorusing, the bodies of these tiny anurans are inflated until nearly spherical. At these times the narrow-mouthed frogs look very much like large marbles equipped with tiny legs and a pointed nose. The males of all these species usually have dark throat skin.

Habits: The calls of these creatures are like the bleating of sheep, with a nasal quality. These frogs seek out temporarily flooded ditches and puddles for breeding and are common in urban areas, although—even when calling—they are secretive and difficult to find. It may take the nocturnal efforts of two persons, triangulating the beams of flashlights on the patch of wet grass from which the calls are being voiced, to find these little animals.

When they are not calling, they are most frequently found by overturning roadside or pondside debris. They seem to especially favor man-made debris, and several may be present beneath decaying boards or dew-dampened cardboard. The ground color of these little frogs often approximates the color of the soil on which they are found.

Diet: Because of the diminutive size of the American microhylids (especially the head), their diet is restricted to the tiniest of insects. Ants, termites, springtails, and the like are consumed in large numbers.

The large Malayan microhylid, Kaloula pulchra, *is commonly called the painted frog. It is a terrestrial burrower but does quite well in captivity.*

Captive care: None of the American microhylids have been captive bred. Indeed, because of their somber colors, small sizes, and restricted diets, few are kept as captives.

When inflated and calling, the tiny common narrow-mouthed toad, Gastrophryne carolinensis, *of our southeastern states, looks like a pointed-nosed marble and sounds like a bleating sheep.*

Useful Addresses and Literature

Periodicals

Reptiles
  P.O. Box 6050
  Mission Viejo, CA 92690

Reptile and Amphibian Magazine
  RD 3, Box 3709-A
  Pottsville, PA 17901

Reptilian
  22 Firs Close, Hazlemere
  High Wycombe, Buck HP15 7HF
  England

The Vivarium (the publication of the American Federation of Herpetoculturists),
  P.O. Box 300067
  Escondido, CA 92030

Arnold, E. N., and J. A. Burton. *A Field Guide to the Reptiles and Amphibians of Britain and Europe.* London: Collins, 1978.

Bartlett, R. D. *In Search of Reptiles and Amphibians.* New York: E. J. Brill, 1988.

—————— *Digest for the Successful Terrarium.* Morris Plains, NJ; TetraPress, 1989.

Cogger, Harold A. *Reptiles and Amphibians of Australia.* Ithaca: Cornell, 1992.

Conant, Roger, and Joseph T. Collins. *Reptiles and Amphibians, Eastern/Central North America.* New York: Houghton Mifflin, 1991.

Duellman, William E., and Linda Trueb. *Biology of Amphibians.* New York: McGraw Hill, 1986.

Halliday, Tim, and Kraig Adler, eds. *The Encyclopedia of Reptiles and Amphibians.* New York: Facts on File, 1986.

Mattison, Chris. *Frogs and Toads of the World.* New York: Facts on File, 1987.

Phillips, Kathryn. *Tracking the Vanishing Frogs.* New York: St. Martin's Press, 1994.

Peters, James A. *Dictionary of Herpetology.* New York: Hafner, 1964.

Schwartz, Albert, and Robert W. Henderson. *Amphibians and Reptiles of the West Indies.* Gainesville, FL: University of Florida Press, 1991.

Slavens, Frank, and Kate Slavens. *Reptiles and Amphibians in Captivity: Breeding, Longevity and Inventory, Current January 1, 1993.* Seattle: Slaveware, 1993.

Smith, Hobart M., and Edward H. Taylor. *Herpetology of Mexico.* Ashton, MD: Eric Lundberg, 1966.

Stebbins, Robert C. *A Field Guide to Western Reptiles and Amphibians.* Boston: Houghton Mifflin, 1985.

Wareham, David C. *The Reptile and Amphibian Keeper's Dictionary.* London: Blandford, 1993.

Tyning, Thomas F. *A Guide to Amphibians and Reptiles.* Boston: Little, Brown & Co., 1990.

Zhao, Er-Mi, and Kraig Adler. *Herpetology of China.* Lawrence, KS: SSAR, 1993.

Glossary

Aestivation A period of warm weather inactivity; often triggered by excessive heat or drought.

Allopatric Not occurring together but often adjacent.

Ambient temperature The temperature of the surrounding environment.

Amplexus The breeding grasp.

Anterior Toward the front.

Anus The external opening of the cloaca; the vent.

Aposematic Brilliantly colored so as to warn predators of toxicity or other danger.

Arboreal Tree-dwelling.

Brumation The reptilian and amphibian equivalent of mammalian hibernation.

Bufonid A toad.

Caudal Pertaining to the tail (with tadpoles).

Cloaca The common chamber into which digestive, urinary, and reproductive systems empty and which itself opens exteriorly through the vent or anus.

Con- A variant of the prefix **com-**, meaning "with" and "in association." (Congeneric refers to species in the same genus, conspecific to the same species.)

Crepuscular Active at dusk or dawn.

Cryptic Fitted for concealing; as used here, having an outline, color, or both, that blends with a specific background.

Dendrobatid An arrow-poison or torrent frog.

Deposition As used here, the act or process of depositing eggs.

Deposition site The spot chosen by the female to lay her eggs.

Dichromatic Exhibiting two color phases within a species; often a sex-linked characteristic.

Dimorphism The occurrence of two forms distinct in build or coloration among animals of the same species; often sex-linked.

Direct development The tadpoles metamorphose within the egg capsule and have no free-swimming aquatic stage.

Diurnal Active in the daytime.

Dorsal Pertaining to the back or upper surface.

Dorsolateral Pertaining to the upper sides.

Dorsolateral ridge A glandular longitudinal ridge on the upper sides of some frogs.

Dorsum The upper surface.

Endemic Confined to a specific region.

Femur The part of the leg between hip and knee.

Form An identifiable species or subspecies.

Fossorial burrowing.

Genus A taxonomic classification of a group of species having similar characteristics. The genus falls between the next higher designation of "family" and the next lower designation of "species." Genera is the singular of genus. The generic name is always capitalized.

Gravid Pregnant.

Gular Pertaining to the throat.

Heliothermic Pertaining to a species that basks in the sun to thermo-regulate.

Hybrid Offspring resulting from the breeding of two species.

Hydrate To restore body moisture by drinking or absorption.

Hydration chamber An enclosed high-humidity chamber used to help desiccated frogs rehydrate.

Hylid A treefrog.

Insular Dwelling on an island.

Intergrade Offspring resulting from the breeding of two subspecies.

Juvenile A young or immature specimen.

Labial Pertaining to the lips.

Lateral Pertaining to the side.

Lateral line organs Sensory organs imbedded in the lateral lines of some aquatic frogs and sensitive to vibrations.

Leptodactylid A member of the anuran family Leptodactylidae.

Lichenate Irregularly edged (usually) darker markings; similar in appearance to the irregular growth pattern of a lichen.

Melanism Condition in which a profusion of black pigment occurs.

Metamorph Baby anuran, recently transformed into the tadpole stage.

Metamorphosis The transformation from one stage of life to another.

Microhylid A narrow-mouthed toad, or its kin.

Middorsal Pertaining to the middle of the back.

Midventral Pertaining to the center of the belly or abdomen.

Monotypic Containing but one type.

Nocturnal Active at night.

Nuptial excrescences The roughened thumb, wrist, and forearm grasping pads of reproductively active male anurans.

Ocelli Dark (or light) edged circular spots (like the spots of an ocelot).

Oviparous Reproducing by means of eggs that hatch after laying.

Ovoviviparous Reproducing by means of shelled or membrane-contained eggs that hatch prior to or at deposition.

Parotoid glands The toxin-producing shoulder glands of toads.

Phalanges The bones of the toes.

Poikilothermic Having no internal regulation of body temperature; cold-blooded.

Pollywog Tadpole.

Posterior Toward the rear.

Phyllomedusine Referring to a treefrog of the subfamily Phyllomedusinae, one of the "monkey" or "leaf" treefrogs.

Race A subspecies.

Ranid A true frog.

Rugose Not smooth; wrinkled or tuberculate.

Saxicolous Rock-dwelling.

Scansorial Capable of or adapted for climbing.

Species A group of similar creatures that produce viable young when breeding. The taxonomic designation that falls beneath genus and above subspecies.

Subdigital Beneath the toes.

Subspecies The subdivision of a species. A race that may differ slightly in color, size, scalation, or other features.

Supratympanal Positioned above the tympanum (external eardrum).

Superciliary positioned on the upper eyelid.

Sympatric Occurring in the same geographical area.

Taxonomy The science of classification of plants and animals.

Terrestrial Land-dwelling.

Thermoregulate To regulate (body) temperature by choosing a warmer or cooler environment.

Thigmothermic Pertaining to a species (often nocturnal) that thermoregulates by being in contact with a warm surface such as a boulder or tarred road-surface.

Tuberculate Having tubercles.

Tubercles Warty protuberances.

Tympanum The external eardrum.

Vent The external opening of the cloaca; the anus.

Venter The underside of a creature; the belly.

Ventral Pertaining to the undersurface or belly.

Ventrolateral Pertaining to the sides of the venter (belly).

The White's treefrog, Litoria caerulea, *a native of Australia, New Guinea and closeby islands, is large, impressive and hardy. It is now bred in large numbers by herpetoculturists.*

Index

Bold face type indicates color photos. **C1** indicates front cover; **C2**, inside front cover; **C3**, inside back cover; **C4**, back cover.

Agalychnis callidryas, 74–77, **76**
Alytes:
  obstetricians, 10, **10**
Aromobates, 64
Ascaphus truei, 9, **9**
Atelopus, 62–63
  flavescens, **61**, 62
  varius, 62

Bombina, 40–43
  bombina, 40
  maxima, 40
  orientalis, **36**, **40**, 40
  variegatus, 40
Breeding, 34–39
  reproductive cycling, 35
Bufo:
  americanus, 7, **60**
  boreas (eggs of), **36**
  debilis, **60**, 61
  marinus, 9, 59–61, **60**
  quercicus, 7, **36**, 59, 61
  retiformis, 16, **16**
Bufonidae, 59–63
Bullfrog, 7, 86–87, **87**

Caging, 16–26 (*also see*
    individual species accounts)
  aquaria, 18–19
  cleanliness, 23
  furnishings, 22–23
  indoor, 17–21
  lighting, 24–25
  microenvironment, 16–17
  outdoor, 22
  terraria, 19–21
    semiaquatic, 19–20
    solid land, 20
    woodland, 20–21
  watering, 26
Calls, 7
Ceratophryinae, 52–58
Ceratophrys, 52–55
  aurita, 54
  calcarata, **53**, 55, 55
  cornuta, **53**, **54**, 55
  cranwelli, **53**, **54**, 55, **C3**
  ornata, **52**, **54**, 54–55
Chacophrys pierotti, 17, 56, **57**

Colostethus, 64
Conraua:
  goliath, 9

Dendrobates, 64
  auratus, 67, **68**, 69, **C4** (top right)
  azureus, **68**, 70
  fantasticus, 67
  granuliferus, 67
  histrionicus, 67, **68**, 70
  leucomelas, **68**, 68
  pumilio, **64**, 64–65, 67, 68
  quinquevittatus, 67
  reticulatus, **64**, 67, **C4** (bottom left)
  speciosus, 67
  tinctorius, 67, **69**, 70
  ventrimaculatus, 67
Dendrobatidae, 64–73
Diets, 27–31
  insects, 27–31
    crickets, 28–29
    fruit flies, 31
    grasshoppers/locusts, 29
    houseflies, 31
    mealworms, 30
    mice, 31
    roaches, 30
    termites, 30
    waxworms, 29
Discoglossidae, 40–43
Dyscophus, 97–98
  antongili, 97, **98**
  guineti, 97, **98**
  insularis, 97

Epipedobates, 64
  tricolor, 67, **69**, 70, **72**, **73**
Escuerzo, 52

Family tree, 11
Frog:
  African bullfrog (*see* pyxie frogs)
  African clawed (*see* clawed frogs)
  arrow-poison, 21
    bicolored, 7, **9**, 66
    black and yellow, 68, **68**
    blue, **68**, 70
    blue and yellow, **69**, 70
    dyeing (*see* blue and yellow)

  gold-banded, 66
  golden, 66
  Golfodulcean, **69**, 70
  green and black, **68**, 69, **C4**
    (top right)
  harlequin, **68**, 70
  phantasmal, **69**, 70, **72**, **73**
  reticulated, **64**, **C4** (bottom left)
  strawberry, **65**, 65–66
Asian cascade, **4**, 89, **89**
bronze, 7
Budgett's, 17, **56**, 56
Chacoan burrowing, 17, 56, **57**
clawed, 18, 19, 44–47
Darwin's, 10, **10**
dwarf underwater, 18, 19, **44**,
    44–47
Freddie Kruger, 56
gastric-brooding, 10, 12
green, 7, **8**
Goliath, 9
hairy, **8**, 9
harlequin, 62–63
  golden, **61**, 62
  variable, 62
horned, 17, 52–55
  Argentine (*see* ornate)
  Brazilian, 54
  Chacoan, **53**, **54**, 55
  Colombian, **53**, 55
  Cranwell's (*see* Chacoan)
  hybrids, 55
  Malayan, **49**, 51
  ornate, **52**, **54**, 54–55
  Surinam, **53**, **54**, 55
Lake Titicaca, 3
leopard
  American, 89
  northern, 12
  southern, **89**
Malayan painted, 98, **99**
ornate, **52**, 54, **C4** (bottom right)
Pac-man, 52
pig, 88–89
Puerto Rican white-lipped, 9
pyxie, 87–88, **88**, **C4** (top left)
  dwarf, 88
red-legged, 12, 86
rocket, 64

sheep, 98–99
skunk, 64
strawberry, **65**
tailed, 9, **9**
Tarahumara, 12
tomato, 97–98
    common, 97, **98**
    Guinet's, 97, **98**
    western, 97
turtle, 9
white-lipped, 9
wood, 9, 90, **90**
yellow-legged, 12, 86

*G*astrophryne sp., 98–99
    carolinensis, **99**
Gastrotheca sp., 10, **10**
    marsupiatum, 12

Health, 32–33
    diseases, 32–33 (*also see*
        individual species accounts)
    hints, 32
    hygiene, 32
Hydration chamber, 26
Hyla:
    andersonii, 7, **8**
    arenicolor, **85**, 85
    avivoca, 85
    chrysoscelis, 7, **85**, 85
    cinerea, **83**, 84
    gratiosa, **83**, 84
    versicolor, **C2**, 7, 84
Hylidae, 74–85
Hymenochirus curtipes, **44**, 44–47
Hypopachus, 98–99

*K*aloula pulchra, 98, **99**

*L*epidobatrachus, 56
    asper, 56
    laevis, 56, **56**
    llanensis, 56
Leptodactylidae, 52–58
Leptodactylus:
    albilabris, 9
    nigroventris, 12
Litoria:
    caerulea, **C1**, **77**, 77–81
    infrafrenata, **81**, 81–82

Mantella, 21, 90–96
    arboreal, 92–93
    brown, **94**, 94
    golden, **91**, 91–92, **92**
    green, **93**, 93
    mystery, **93**
    orange-banded, **94**, 94

painted, **92**, 92
saffron, **93**, 93
Mantella, 21, 90–96
    aurantiaca, **91**, 91–92, **92**
    betsileo, **94**, 94
    cowani, **94**, 94
    crocea, **93**
    expectata, 93–94
    laevigata, 92–93
    madagascariensis, **92**, 92
    "mysteriosa," **93**, 93
    viridis, **93**
Melanophryniscus stelzneri, **61**, 61
Megophrys nasuta, **49**, 51
Microhylidae, 97–99
Minyobates, 64
Myobatrachus:
    gouldii, 9

*O*steopilus septentrionalis, **82**, 82–83
    eggs of, **36**

*P*edostibes hosei, 59, **60**
Pelobatidae, 49–51
Photographing, 13–15
Phyllobates, 64, 66
    aurotaenia, 66
    bicolor, 9, **9**, 66
    terribilis, 66
    vittatus, 67, **69**, 70
Pipa pipa, 47–48, **48**
Pipidae, 44–48
Polliwogs (*see* tadpoles)
Psyllophryne:
    didactyla, 9
Pyxicephalus adspersus, 87–88, **88**,
    C4 (top left)
    delalandei, 88

*R*ana:
    aurora, 86
    catesbeiana, 7, 86–87, **88**
    clamitans, 7, **8**
    grylio, 88–89
    livida, **4**, 89, **89**
    muscosa, 86
    *pipiens (*complex), 89–90
    sylvatica, 9, 90, **90**
    (*utricularia*) *sphenocephala*, 89, **89**
Ranidae, 86–96
Rheobatrachus:
    silus, 10
    vitellinus, 10
Rhinoderma:
    darwinii, 10, **10**

*S*caphiopus:
    h. holbrooki, **49**, 50–51

Sminthillus:
    limbatus, 9
Spadefoot:
    Couch's, 7
    eastern, **49**, 50–51
    western, 7
Spea, 50
Spindly-leg syndrome, 0
Tadpoles, 4–39
Taxonomy, 11
Telmatobius:
    culeus, 9
Terrariums, 16–26
Toad:
    American, 7, **60**
    arboreal, 59
    Argentine flame-bellied, **61**,
        62
    common green, **60**, 61
    European midwife, 10, **10**
    fire-bellied, 18, 40–43
        European, 40, **41**
        Oriental, **36**, 40, 40
    Fowler's, 7
    giant, 9, 59–61, **60**
    golden, 12
    ground dwelling, 59
    Malayan climbing, 59, **60**
    narrow-mouthed, 98–99
        eastern, **99**
    oak, 7, **36**, 59
    Sonoran green, 16, **16**, 61
    Surinam, 18, 19, 47–48, **48**
    United States (of the), 59–62
    western (eggs of), **36**
    Wyoming, 12
    yellow-bellied, 40, **41**
Treefrog:
    barking, **83**, 84
    bird-voiced, 85
    canyon, **85**, 85
    Cuban, **82**, 82–83
        eggs of, **36**
    green, 7, **83**, 84
    gray, **C2**, 7, **84**, 84–85
    marsupial, 10, **10**, **12**
    pine barrens, 7, **8**
    red-eyed, 74–77, **76**
    squirrel, 7
    white-lipped, **81**, 81–82
    White's, **C1**, 18, **77**, 77–81
Trichobatrachus:
    robustus, **8**, 9

Vocalizations, 7

*X*enopus laevis, 44–47, **45**, **47**